LEADERSHIP
TO THE
FIFTH POWER

L⁵

LEADERSHIP TO THE FIFTH POWER

A PRACTICAL MODEL FOR ACCELERATING YOUR
LEADERSHIP CAPACITY TO A HIGHER LEVEL

INCLUDES THE 5TH POWER LEADERSHIP
DEVELOPMENT TOOL
LARRY M. BAIDER

iUniverse, Inc.
New York Lincoln Shanghai

Leadership to the Fifth Power
A Practical Model For Accelerating Your Leadership Capacity To A Higher Level

Copyright © 2007 by Larry M. Baider

All rights reserved. No part of this book may be used or reproduced by any means, graphic, electronic, or mechanical, including photocopying, recording, taping or by any information storage retrieval system without the written permission of the publisher except in the case of brief quotations embodied in critical articles and reviews.

iUniverse books may be ordered through booksellers or by contacting:

iUniverse
2021 Pine Lake Road, Suite 100
Lincoln, NE 68512
www.iuniverse.com
1-800-Authors (1-800-288-4677)

The views expressed in this work are solely those of the author and do not necessarily reflect the views of the publisher, and the publisher hereby disclaims any responsibility for them.

ISBN-13: 978-0-595-39606-1 (pbk)
ISBN-13: 978-0-595-84024-3 (cloth)
ISBN-13: 978-0-595-84009-0 (ebk)
ISBN-10: 0-595-39606-2 (pbk)
ISBN-10: 0-595-84024-8 (cloth)
ISBN-10: 0-595-84009-4 (ebk)

Printed in the United States of America

*To all of my family and friends,
whom I truly appreciate:*

Thank you for being there.

*To the Three Kings,
All-In!*

CONTENTS

Preface ix

Introduction xi

How to Use the Book xvii

Leadership Philosophy 1

Organizational Viewpoints on Leadership Development 5

The Leader's Bonding Agents: The Glue that Binds 11

    The First Ingredient: Choice 13

    The Second Ingredient: Awareness 15

The 5 Powers: A Progressive Leadership Model 17

    The First Power: Vision 19

    The Second Power: Focus 36

    The Third Power: Attitude 50

    The Fourth Power: Relating 66

    The Fifth Power: Developing 82

Leadership in Action 97

Leadership Capacity: Measuring Your Success 111

Driving Leadership Capacity 113

Conclusion 119

Appendix A: Driving Leadership Capacity—Pocket Version ...121

Appendix B: The 5th Power Tool 127

    Introduction 127

    Instructions for Use 128

    Leadership Capacity Scorecard 135

Leadership Development Plan 136
References 139
Index 143

PREFACE

As my daughter's simple insight demonstrates, leadership doesn't have to be complicated. On one of the many evenings that I worked on writing this book, I was tending to my fatherly ritual of saying good night to my children as they went to bed. One night in particular, my daughter Kyra, who was seven at the time, had a brief but incredibly insightful exchange with me as I prepared to leave her room. It went like this:

"Dad, why are you leaving my room so quickly?"

"Well, I'm trying really hard to finish my book on leadership," I said.

"Oh, that's right, your book on leadership. You're a good leader, but I don't really lead anyone," she said.

"You know, Kyra, you do actually lead someone, and that someone is you. And you know what? That's the most important person you can lead, because if you can't lead yourself, you can't lead other people."

She listened patiently as I preached from my soapbox and just kept looking at me. Then I said, "You know, Kyra, you're a good leader because you do lead yourself well. So how do you do it?"

In her typical wise-beyond-her-years manner, she said, "Well, Dad, I guess I follow my heart."

You can only imagine how I stopped in my tracks, struck by that insightful remark. I looked back at her and said, "You know, you're right. Leadership really does have something to do with following your heart."

And then she threw me the knockout punch and said, "No, Dad, it has everything to do with your heart."

Although leadership might seem and feel complicated at times, there are simple, strategic steps that you can take in order to make high-impact leadership less random and more sustainable.

Whether you're a veteran leader of a large organization, an emerging leader of a new work team, or somewhere in between, the principles and model outlined in this book will lay the groundwork to significantly accelerate your leadership capacity.

The five tenets—referred to as the "5 Powers"—along with elements referred to as "the glue," make the process of becoming a more effective leader tangible. This book doesn't merely focus the reader on what leaders have to accomplish in their roles, nor does it outline all of the characteristics that leaders must possess in order to be effective. This book drives home the behaviors, competencies, and tenets that leaders need to develop and continually refine in order to experience sustained success. Applying these fundamentals and learning to self-audit your leadership capacity will make a dramatic difference in how you lead both yourself and others.

INTRODUCTION

Leadership is like a puzzle in the following respect. We take pieces that are on the table, try to fit them together, remove those that clearly don't fit, and then try to find the right connection with other pieces. Some pieces fit with great ease, and others take more time. However, once the pieces are together, the puzzle is complete. There's no need to keep fitting the pieces together to complete the picture. When it's done, it's done.

This is where the analogy ends. More accurately stated, the analogy comes to a grinding halt, because unlike constructing a puzzle, the pieces in leadership keep shifting and changing, and often do so rather quickly. With the pieces changing in size, shape, and position so frequently, the "leadership puzzle" never quite looks the same.

Leadership, and learning to lead, is an incredibly dynamic process. And while most of us recognize that we're dealing with people and not machines, we're often amazed, surprised, and at times frustrated when the pieces don't fit so easily.

The potential for leadership exists everywhere and, some might argue, within everyone. It's more overtly observed and scrutinized within our government, our communities, and our workplaces. The various media outlets available today have exposed numerous examples of blatantly poor and irresponsible leadership practices, leaving many to ask, "What makes someone a good leader?"

Though leadership can and does exist everywhere, there's often an aura of elusiveness surrounding the very topic.

However, there's one thing we can't deny—we all know great leadership when we see it. When we're in the presence of highly effective leaders, we become inspired. Powerful leaders know how to motivate and bring out the very best in people. They use the right words, make decisions with conviction, and take clear courses of action. Not only do great leaders know how to connect with others; they also possess the ability to demystify situations that are otherwise unclear and quell fear of the unknown.

So here are two pivotal questions:

- Why is it so challenging for many in formal positions of leadership to "act" like good leaders?
- Why is it so difficult to sustain effective leadership performance, even for those already considered effective leaders?

Let's start with question two first. I'd suggest that effective leadership is sustainable, and that it doesn't have to be random. It's more available than we often recognize, but we must acknowledge that it is not a one-and-done event. It is, in fact, a process, and an ongoing, lengthy one at that. It requires a tremendous degree of commitment to sharpen and an abundance of personal maturity to implement. You have to be willing to look in the mirror and ask difficult questions. Again, you don't just "get it" one day and then stop learning and developing as a leader. Therefore, it becomes much clearer why sustainability issues surface around leadership effectiveness. And while the diligence required is significant, the benefits are unparalleled.

In attempting to answer the first question, there exists a host of possibilities. We certainly have to consider that there are some individuals in formal leadership positions who simply become intoxicated with "position," and end up abusing the formal power they've been granted. Even with the purest of intentions, some tend to veer off track more easily than others. The reasons for these diversions are too many to discuss, and are not our focus here.

The third and possibly most prominent factor for failing to act like good leaders boils down to how we define management and leadership. I suggest this has been a long-standing point of confusion in terms of their application to frontline practice. That is, "management" has often been lumped together with leadership, and generally with little or no distinction between the two. Even today, this lack of understanding and blurring of the lines often results in the best technicians in an industry or profession being thrust into leadership roles for which they're ill-prepared. We've all observed or have been caught up in this dynamic. For example, the most responsible or technically inclined nurse becomes the team leader or unit manager. The most efficient professional services manager in a firm is promoted to partner even though he or she is severely lacking in the ability to communicate a working vision or relate to his or her constituency.

Without proper training and learning, both the people in formal positions of leadership and their constituents experience less-than-favorable outcomes. The constituent experiences extended durations of frustration that eventually lead to doubt and faith in the leader. Hence, there are missed opportunities to formulate progressive teams and function in a high-performance mode. The unprepared leader also experiences extended periods of self-doubt, further diminishing their performance and effectiveness. As a result the individual who earlier demonstrated leadership potential may forever opt out of this direction and end up in the land of the lost leaders.

Organizations as a whole don't fare that well, either. The byproducts of poor leadership are many. They range from substandard performance due to poorly directed and under inspired workforces all the way to excessive turnover rates that prove to be costly to any organization. Losing employees as a result of sub par or lackluster leadership is a standard that no organization should be willing to accept. It's bad for morale with internal constituents, bad for the company's reputation externally, and, quite frankly, it's bad for the bottom line.

In order for organizations to experience sustained success, competent management and leadership must both be present among their employees—the critical point being, they are needed within the same people. That's right, organizations need those in formal positions of management to be both good managers *and* good leaders. Proficiency in organization and planning is simply not enough to compensate for inadequacy in communicating vision and relating to others. It is only when we embrace the fact that both leadership and management must exist under the same roof that we begin to experience the success desired.

So as we dive into the L5 model, let's do so with the earnest belief that leadership doesn't have to remain elusive and beyond our grasp. Becoming a good, or even great, leader is as possible for you as it was for the leaders you've admired and respected.

HOW TO USE THE BOOK

After reading the opening sections—which I encourage you to read first, as they set the foundation—you'll enter into the thick of the L5 model. Along with exploration of each of the five leadership powers, I'll explain what are referred to as sticking points.

The term *sticking point* sounds like it should refer to those instances in which we're being held back or limited by some impeding factor. In the 5th Power, sticking points are quite the opposite—they are the ingredients that matter most. These key points are the elements that I want to "stick" with you as you enter and continue on the path of personal and leadership development. Tapping into these sticking points is how you enhance your abilities. We will refer to this overarching ability as your *leadership capacity,* or "LC."

Toward the back of the book, you will find examples of leadership challenges along with suggested solutions. You will also find a recap of the sticking points for easy reference. Following the recap is the "5th Power" tool. This will guide you in determining areas of strength and weakness, and will pave the foundation for your individual leadership development plan. Keep in mind the process is dynamic, and the plan should evolve as you hone your abilities.

If you have an executive, personal, or leadership coach, I suggest you consider integrating the goals and plan you develop into your coaching sessions.

LEADERSHIP PHILOSOPHY

To establish some additional groundwork, let's highlight some philosophical perspectives that are both reasonable and highly relevant.

• Leaders Are, in Fact, Created

This speaks to the age-old debate over whether leaders are born or are created. While some individuals seem to have a natural propensity for leading, developing varying degrees of proficiency in leadership is within almost everyone's grasp. The key ingredients to attaining this skill seem to be desire and awareness.

• Leadership Development Is Personal Development

It's impossible to develop as a leader without developing as a person. The skills and qualities that mold, define, and fortify high-quality leadership occur at an inner core. One cannot authentically become a more effective leader by simply working on superficial tactics and techniques to improve his or her leadership capabilities. Sustained effectiveness is only realized when you start to clean up your own backyard and not someone else's. It's only when you become a more effective leader of yourself that you can become a more effective leader of others.

• Simply Having People Follow Your Path Doesn't Make You a Great Leader

Another topic that often inspires great debate is whether simply rallying others behind your cause and inspiring them to follow constitutes being a "good" leader. Communicating a counterproductive, self-serving, or even destructive message or vision—even if you manage to get people to buy into it—simply means you have the ability to inspire people to follow. Good and great leaders have messages that serve a greater good, and are usually more inclusive, rather than exclusive, of others.

• Leadership Development Is Not a Linear Process

You don't simply become a good leader and stop developing; ongoing and deliberate cultivation will be required. There are numerous factors that push and pull on each of us, day-in and day-out. When in formal positions of leadership, that pushing and pulling seems to become magnified. Being a good leader is a lifelong journey.

• Organizational Effectiveness Is Proportional to Its Bench Leadership

Even without great leadership, an organization can post profits and grow within its particular industry. However, organizations that continue to operate with poor or underdeveloped leaders suffer and lose out in other vital aspects that drive mid- and long-range capabilities. Organizations need a number of individuals who are capable of leading. Too often, however, team benches are short on "doers." Leaders must learn to expand the bench and develop other leaders. This is not only good people strategy—it's also good business strategy.

• Though Leadership and Management Skill Sets Are Very Different, Organizations Need Both in the Same People

Leadership and management are different. Though the terms are often used interchangeably, the skills themselves differ. While management is about a formal position, leadership is about your *disposition*. Another way of looking at this is to say management is about your position and what has to get done, while leadership is how you go about doing it.

ORGANIZATIONAL VIEWPOINTS ON LEADERSHIP DEVELOPMENT

Culture is the life-thread and glue that links our past, present, and future.

—J. W. Marriott Jr.

There are a number of variables that influence whether organizations invest the resources necessary to develop their leadership teams. The following are typical questions, concerns, and beliefs that one might possess with regard to the development process:

- It's hard enough to tackle everyday job responsibilities, let alone work on becoming a better leader.
- Becoming a more effective leader requires a lot of energy.
- It gets lonely being the leader.
- The responsibility of making difficult decisions that affect everyone can be very stressful and, at times, overwhelming.
- Our company simply does not have the money and time required to bolster our leadership team.

These are all valid concerns. It does require time, it does require energy, and there is an inherent risk that comes along with critical decision-making. However, we are not going to develop as leaders, nor are our organizations going to excel, if we subscribe to the belief that it's not worth the effort. Organizations will never realize their true potential if they don't make the investment in human capital (i.e., people).

Although there are various perspectives on the value of leadership development, I'd like to touch on what I believe are the four most commonly held beliefs. On one end of the scale is the belief that the development process is the proverbial "soft stuff," in that it's fluff and not really essential to the success of the business. Essentially, people of this mind-set believe it doesn't add anything to the bottom line. At the opposite end of the spectrum is the recognition that development is the very foundation and core of an organization's success. These organizations learn how to tie development into performance goals, and learning into business strategy.

Somewhere in the middle of the scale, we find two similar perspectives, though with slight variation. There are organizations that are willing to commit the time and money, but somehow fall short on sustaining execution. More specifically, these companies are often willing to allocate significant funding toward the development of their leaders by sending people on expensive retreats or to elaborate seminars that "teach" leadership. Now there's absolutely nothing wrong with this approach to developing leaders, but too often the material is never reinforced and integrated into the leader's arsenal for long-term success and sustainability. Essentially, the training rarely transfers into learning.

Finally, there are those organizations that appear to recognize the positive impact that training has on the bottom line, but they fail to stay the course. More specifically, there's a wavering commitment level in less than ideal times. In these organizations we would observe an ebb and flow in commitment to the leadership development process that is inversely proportional to the measure of crisis within the company.

⇑ Levels of Organizational Crisis = ⇓ Emphasis of Development
and
⇓ Levels of Organizational Crisis = ⇑ Attention to Development

When things are on an even keel and crises are experienced at lower intensities, top management is more likely to commit the time and money to the leadership development process. In contrast, when crises are on the rise, the time allotted, money allocated, and energy expended into developing the company's leaders tend to go by the wayside.

This sets the stage for a rather paradoxical circumstance: when organizational commitment to development remains constant, derailing and spiraling into crisis mode occurs less frequently. On the other hand, when an organization contracts its efforts every time a crisis occurs, it's literally like starting over time and time again.

Even if you already consider yourself an effective leader, you know that you still struggle at times. It's quite normal to sometimes feel like we're coming unglued or succumbing to mounting pressure. Derailing can be the result of a single, but significant, incident, or the result of cumulative factors. In either respect, we may lose our ability to be effective.

Our test as leaders doesn't come when the waters are quiet and still; it's the rough waves that expose our true leadership abilities. Adversity certainly has a way of revealing the strengths—and the weaknesses—that we each possess.

For those of you functioning as leaders at any level within an organization, you know that all eyes are on you at all times. Your abilities and actions are being observed regularly and with great interest. The manner in which you respond to challenges, drive change, and relate to others will define you as a leader among your constituents over time.

And let's not forget the significance of quality and richness, both in and outside of the workplace. The more effective you are as a leader, the more satisfied you will be in every aspect of your life. You learn to be more present minded, more focused, and you get more out of every experience. You enjoy—yes, actually enjoy—what you're "doing," as opposed to defaulting to autopilot mode and simply going through the motions. When you become a more effective leader, you can, and most certainly will, positively influence and impact those around you.

One final thought with respect to leadership is worth mentioning. Your development as a leader should never be left up to, or be dependent on, the willingness of an organization, a manager, or the board to whom you report. If an organization chooses to make that commitment, consider it a bonus. If, however, they don't make that formal commitment, then it's up to you to make development a priority for yourself. In either case, the real commitment begins internally—with you—and only you can make leadership development a reality.

THE LEADER'S BONDING AGENTS:
THE GLUE THAT BINDS

While effective leadership is dependent upon a number of characteristics, we will focus on five areas that I believe are critical for sustained development. In addition to the *powers*, there is what I call *the glue*. This bonding agent holds the powers together, and is composed of *choice* and *awareness*.

We will refer to the combined ingredients as *G2*, as they are the two elements that leaders always possess at the foundation of their thoughts, interactions, and decisions. The challenge is for the leader to exercise these elements regularly, so that they serve themselves and their constituents to the highest caliber.

The model for these agents is:

Choice + Awareness = G2

The First Ingredient: Choice

In many respects, choice is a state of mind. I suggest that in this context, choice means there is as an absolute, unwavering belief that becoming a more effective leader is always an option. That's right, developing into a better, more effective, and more resilient leader is always, and I mean always, a personal choice. Whether you're leading from the front of the pack, or from the middle, making the choice to be a leader is up to you.

Differences in style aside, when you are on the journey to becoming a more evolved leader, you make things happen by choice. Leadership, like so many other aspects of life, is not a spectator sport. In too many situations, we can observe what I call sideline leadership. This is when those in formal positions of leadership come off the playing field and decide to stand on the sidelines. Instead of remaining on the field when the going gets tough, or acknowledging it's time to step up and assume responsibility, they decide they'd rather watch from where it's ultimately safe. That's not what your constituents or peers expect from you as a leader. They expect—and rightly so—that you'll be right there beside them, or better yet, out in front of them, paving the path through sound example.

Leaders make things happen, and they do so by

- accepting responsibility for their actions, instead of blaming others or passing the buck;
- looking out for the welfare of others in addition to their own;

- living purpose-driven lives;
- clarifying intentions and expectations for themselves and those they serve;
- making the difficult decisions that others most often don't want to make.

The fact that we, as individuals, have choices available to us in almost every situation is often lost. Why does this happen, especially when we learn early on in our lives that we have to face consequences for our actions? Further, how do we change these behaviors?

The Second Ingredient: Awareness

This leads us to our second ingredient, awareness. In order to become more willing to accept responsibility for our actions, develop more genuine interest in others, live with greater purpose, and act on clear intentions, we have to raise our awareness levels.

This is only possible when we take measures to become more cognizant of our actions. We must create the opportunity and space to think about our actions by slowing down and applying the brakes—not slamming on the brakes, just simply decelerating. Though it sometimes seems impossible, it really is within our grasp more times than not. It requires that we slow our responses down a notch or two.

Here are some sample workplace questions that you can ask yourself as you're attempting to apply the brakes:

- Was I open to the feedback my team offered when they questioned the strategy I proposed?
- Did I seize the opportunity to convey my vision to the team?
- Did I spend time and energy on things that steered me off course and away from my goals?
- Did I set the type of example that I wanted to during the meeting?

You simply cannot be an effective leader if your actions are frenetic, disjointed, and without some reasonable degree of thought. Obviously, spontaneous responses are often required from leaders. We see this most often when a crisis occurs and a rapid response is the only option. On that very note, one could argue that as we train ourselves to become more proficient in managing smaller crises, we are simultaneously preparing ourselves to tackle larger and more serious crises.

The bottom line is this: you have to create the time to process, filter, and learn from your decisions and interactions.

These two ingredients—choice and awareness—form the bonding agent that consistently acts on and within each of the 5 Powers.

THE 5 POWERS:
A PROGRESSIVE LEADERSHIP MODEL

This section of the book explains the detailed L5 model. The 5 Powers are explained within the context of a foundation, followed by the sticking points that solidify each of the powers.

The Five Powers

The First Power: Vision

The Second Power: Focus

The Third Power: Attitude

The Fourth Power: Relating

The Fifth Power: Developing

The First Power

Vision

Highly effective leaders understand how to create clarity so that everyone moves along the path with reasonable expectation.

The Foundation

What is vision, and why is it so imperative for leaders to understand its application?

Vision is the ability to see, and, within the context we're discussing, to see into the future. It's the ability to create a mental picture that reflects a future state, and in many cases, to communicate that future state to other people.

That is a key point to highlight: Vision is the ability to reflect and communicate a future state of being.

While the distance or range to which we are able to envision may certainly be influenced by a number of factors, it's vital that we appreciate and understand its parallel to our level of effectiveness. Cooper and Sawaf (1997) refer to this distance as a *time horizon*, and imply that the range of this horizon—be it limited or expansive—effects work capacity and performance. Specifically, they indicate that individuals displaying more limited time horizons tend to overreact to minor problems, while those with ability to exercise greater horizons respond to complexity and chaos much more effectively.

In order to fully appreciate the importance that vision plays in leadership, we must first consider and acknowledge that it exists in various forms. Vision and the visioning process can occur on a personal level, within work teams, or, more globally, within the structure of an organization, and each would look something like the following:

- Personal level—whereby an individual envisions a future state of life, personal goals, etc.

- Team level—in which a group or team of individuals share in an anticipated state for which they are striving
- Organizational level—in which the organization as a whole strives to reach a formally agreed-upon state

VISION RING

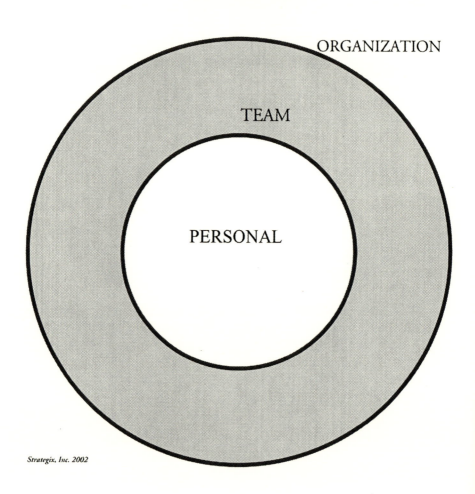

Vision, like leadership itself, tends to occur in levels or rings. We can use and develop vision on a personal level, a team level, and an organizational level. For purposes of application of vision, we will further refine the classifications to macro and micro levels.

The Macro Level

If you work in a corporation, or organization of any size for that matter, you most likely have a vision statement. The statement is often framed and hanging on a common wall for all to see. Whether it is taken seriously and embraced by the employees or the organization's leaders—most likely the crafters of the statement—is, however, another story.

Although the original intent of such statements is to rally the workforce toward a common purpose and paint a picture of the future, the message often gets lost along the way. Buried in bureaucracy or clouded over in business-as-usual policies, the statements themselves lose their impact and possess little to no meaning for the organization's constituency at large.

Therefore, many employees become disillusioned, causing faith in the common purpose to rapidly wane. In time, even the mention of the word "vision" tends to create a pit in one's stomach. One can appreciate, then, how imperative it becomes not only for vision to be created, but also for the organization's leaders to massage the vision deep into its various layers.

This is accomplished through ongoing communication around the vision itself, the inclusion of as many people as possible in vision development, and the willingness of the leadership to exercise consistent behaviors and practices that support and uphold the vision.

The Micro Level

On this level, we're referring to a more personal or team-driven vision. This could range from establishing a set of strategic goals and objectives for our department to charting a new course for personal achievement. In order to use vision as a tool and make it a practical process, we'll need to expand our understanding of the term. Let's also consider using the term *envision*, so that we literally bring the process of creating and driving vision to an action state. When you envision, you create a mental image of something that you see for yourself, your team, or, on the macro level, your organization.

For example, you envision your work team producing on a new level or you envision them exceeding the objectives you've set. What I'm suggesting at this micro level is that you seize these mental images—the vision you see in your mind's eye—and find a way to bring these images to reality. This is really no different than what's accomplished at a corporate retreat, when an organization decides to create or re-create its vision. At the micro level, you are conducting your very own retreat, to latch onto a vision and set a new direction.

When you raise your awareness levels to the process of "envisioning," the direction and actions you take are less random. Similar to leadership itself, the ability to cultivate vision is within our grasp. There are certainly those individuals who have a greater propensity to see and create images of a new landscape and provide directions for getting there. This doesn't mean, however, that you cannot and should not do the same.

In order to be an effective leader, you must possess the ability to both create vision—even if in a varying capacity—and communicate that vision. Your people—whether you refer to them as employees, stakeholders, associates, or constituents—are looking to you, their leader, to do just that—lead. As the leader, you are tasked with the responsibility of shining light on this path called the future through effectively creating, communicating, and driving the vision.

Vision

Sticking Points

- Make Envisioning a Habit

- Communicate Vision with Serious Impact

- Leverage Vision to Inspire, Not Motivate

- Align Vision and Strategy to Drive Change

- Respect the Vision-Values Tie-In

1. Make the Envisioning Process a Habit

In order to effectively use vision as a leadership tool, most of us need to cultivate the process. Even those who appear to be natural visionaries create some reasonable degree of space to develop these thoughts. More often than not, most of us possess the ability to build on these mental images or visions of a future state. For example, when we verbalize an expectation, a goal, or a future state to our work team, we see an image of this verbalized state.

Think about it—we usually see this picture in our mind's eye as we're verbalizing the vision. These mental pictures either come naturally, or we have to make time and space to cultivate them. Before we can tend the garden, we must first grow the garden. In the same manner as tending a garden, we must set aside the necessary time to grow the garden. We need to train ourselves to develop the "envisioning" process.

A perfect starting point is asking these questions of our teams and ourselves: Where do we see ourselves in the next two years? What do we see ourselves accomplishing? How will we look different than we do now? What do we want to stand for in terms of our values, services, etc.?

The purpose of these questions is to envision both what the desired future will look like and how the aspirations of the team or the organization might be realized.

The Glue: Carve out time to make visioning a practice. Shift from random to intentional envisioning.

2. Communicate Vision with Serious Impact

The realization of your vision has much to do with execution and, since we're often involving others, powerful communication.

Communicating vision requires consideration, and should not be haphazard. A philosophy that I strongly encourage you not to adopt is that communicating vision poorly is better than not communicating one at all. When delivering the messages that communicate your vision, consider the intent and exercise precision.

Effective delivery of vision requires that you consider your stakeholders. Who are stakeholders? These are the individuals or groups to whom, or for whom, you're responsible in the scope of your constituency. Critical to the stakeholder is the realization that the delivery of your message—though the vision itself is the same—requires special consideration, depending upon which stakeholder group you're addressing. For example, delivering your vision and key messages to your board of directors, the executive committee, or the town council should sound different than the delivery to your direct reports or managers of other functional areas or departments. Specifically what's different is the "what's in it for me" component. Even with the best of intentions, your stakeholders are listening to your message with considerable degrees of self-interest. Each stakeholder wants to know how your vision will impact them, how they will be included, and yes, maybe even what they're going to get out of the message.

Of equal importance, your vision should clarify direction, intentions, and expectations. It's important to keep in mind that one of your primary roles as a leader is to generate clarity for your constituents. Achieving this through vision is a very powerful and productive mechanism.

The Glue: Communicate your vision with conviction and clarity. Take stock of your "stakeholder Rolodex."

3. Leverage Vision to Inspire, Not Motivate

One of the most important ways in which you can serve your constituents is to shed light on and clarify everyday experiences. Everyday situations that we, as leaders, might view as business as usual can be rather unnerving experiences for our constituents. Even if a high level of trust exists and inclusion is more often the norm, the effective and regular communication of vision is very important for your constituency.

When you communicate vision with regularity, you quell fears and take the opportunity to set direction. Even when you have the best-developed plans and most efficient teams, you need to redirect at times. On a personal level, each time you communicate your vision to others, you're reinforcing that same vision and feeding it the fuel it needs to keep burning.

As a leader, using vision to reset the sights is a powerful practice. You offer reassurance and keep team members working in unison.

It is very important that those in formal positions of leadership appreciate the degree to which people look to them for direction. Even within those organizations that possess strong multilevel leadership, employees seek understanding about direction and the courses being charted. Whether the talent bench is short or deep, leaders should be using vision to inspire and connect with their employees and their constituencies at large.

Remember, communicating vision to inspire doesn't have to involve bells and whistles. In addition to the more formal venues, weave vision into the more casual daily conversations. You will most likely find this strategy to be more natural, more genuinely received, and ultimately more effective when aiming to garner, buy-in, and inspire teams toward more sustained changes that literally transform landscapes. In doing so, you're creating heightened connectivity in that you're sharing the vision on a more personal and meaningful level.

The Glue: Use vision to create a clear picture of desired future states, reduce fear of the unknown, and inspire others to greater heights.

4. Align Vision and Strategy to Drive Change

If you've ever wondered why even the best of ideas often seem to fail to realize their potential, or completely flatline once the planning meetings are over, just ask this follow-up question: Did we tie our strategic and tactical goals into our vision?

In order to drive any degree of change, it becomes important to make sure we align our vision with meaningful goals—be they global goals of the organization, specific frontline goals of a team, or personal goals for your own development and achievement.

If our vision is clear but our goals are vague, then achieving our vision is highly unlikely. If our vision is clear and our goals clearly defined, we stand a much greater chance of realizing our vision. I say much greater chance to achieve rather than guaranteed to achieve for a reason, especially as it relates to team and organizational vision. Even if we embrace this vital concept of vision-goal tie-in, we have to go a step further.

When we are earnestly attempting to achieve a vision in any of the realms we're discussing (i.e., organizational, team, or personal), we are most often talking about driving change. New and desired visions are change processes in the making. Therefore, in addition to clear vision and defined related goals, we need to generate energy around vision and goals. The amount of energy needed to drive vision is usually significant in that we have to provide Psychology Safety (Schein, 2000) for our constituents. Schein says, "This safety allows others to see the possibility of solving problems without losing integrity or identity." Therefore, in order for others to accept, appreciate, and buy into our vision—even if we've included others in the process—we have to demonstrate that there's security and value in the newly designed change initiative.

We do this by generating a sense of urgency. John Kotter (1995) explains that, in general, over 50 percent of change efforts fail due to a lack of urgency. He further states, "Without a vision, the urgency of change can create diminished motivation and even exit by members if not matched by a compelling notion of what can be."

So essentially, we're marrying together two components—vision and goals—and driving them with a genuine, not contrived, sense of urgency that gives our platform the legs it needs to move us and our team along the path.

The Glue: Vision-driven change requires some degree of urgency in order to engage people and move them into action. Providing psychological safety shows them you care about their stake in that change.

5. Respect the Vision-Values Tie-in

We cannot discuss vision in terms of its cultivation, communication, and application without weaving values into the equation.

The decisions we make every day are influenced by a host of variables, and values are a factor in the equation. The manner in which we come to conclusions and filter information has a lot to do with our personal beliefs and our value system.

So what happens when we don't take the time to meditate or enlighten ourselves on our personal values? What happens when we don't set the necessary time aside to figure out what's important to us as individuals when it relates to finding some type of purpose?

Values are often difficult for many of us to articulate unless we've made a concerted effort to explore them. Even if we find it challenging to communicate, or we simply haven't made a habit of exploration, we do know when our personal values are in friction. We've all had the experience of being in a situation where something is unfolding before our eyes that just doesn't feel right. We sense a degree of unease, though we might not even be aware of its source.

When these sometimes ill-defined feelings occur, they're often the result of incongruity between our values and the situation at hand. I'm not suggesting that it's realistic to think that every value will be in direct step with those of our organization or team. What I am suggesting, however, is that when we are more in tune with our personal values and belief systems, we can at least make better sense of everyday situations.

The Glue: Increase awareness around your personal beliefs and values so that you better understand your responses and level of leadership effectiveness.

The Second Power:

Focus

Highly effective leaders do not waste energy on anything that steers them off course.

The Foundation

The second power is focus. This is essentially your ability to stay on point and prioritize your efforts so that you're available for yourself and for others. Why is this so important? Well, most would agree that energy is one of our most precious commodities. When our energy levels are high, we operate with greater confidence and our results are usually more positive.

There's a close link, a marriage of sorts, between time and energy. When you're in a position of leadership, it is critical to maintain your energy in order to make the most of your time. And though we lose energy in various ways, learning to avoid unnecessary depletion is in our best interest.

Leadership requires time, and lots of it. And if you haven't figured it out by now, your constituents want, and need, your time. This precious commodity seems to thin out very rapidly when we're operating in fast-paced environments and under high degrees of pressure.

It's fair to say that most leaders experience intensified constraints with their time. It therefore becomes critical to continuously evaluate how you use and distribute energy in order to remain effective and healthy.

Leaders often deal with highly charged, highly sensitive, and complex issues. Leaders need to focus their energy in order to be effective for themselves and for their constituents. Anyone who has led a group of people knows that it can feel like you're being pulled in any number of directions. Sometimes it feels like everyone wants a piece of you. Every move you make often feels like it's under the microscope.

Effective leaders establish realistic expectations with respect to the amount of time, attention, and energy that is needed by others. We lose considerable energy if we view these everyday occurrences as interruptions or inconveniences in our daily planner.

If we recognize these occurrences as not only an expected but also a valuable aspect of leadership, then we're less disappointed or frustrated when they occur. Accept them as normal day-to-day events that are necessary for connecting to your environment. These are opportunities in the making for you to seem tangible to your constituents.

Focus

Sticking Points

• Adopt the "Nothing Else Matters" Principle

• Avoid the "Everything to Everyone" Trap

• Plug Leaks

• Learn to Anticipate for Focus-Building

• Fill the Tank

1. Adopt the "Nothing Else Matters" Principle

In order to be an effective and proficient leader, it's worthwhile to consider this principle. "Nothing else matters" doesn't mean that you don't care about others, or that you don't care about what's going on outside of your own world. By adopting this sort of mentality, you're actually creating the very time and space that leaders are often lacking as a result of wasting energy on things that really don't matter.

Moving toward our vision, connecting with others, and achieving goals are often impeded or derailed when we focus our time and energy on everyday encounters that take us away from where we want to be. The situations to avoid are those we have no control over and those that are not truly harmful to you or others if left untouched. When it comes to wasted energy, the hill on which you die is always your choice.

Let's think about this in practice and use a rather common example. A colleague makes a comment to you in front of peers during a meeting. While the comment itself may have been vague and indirect, you perceived it nonetheless as unflattering. Your choices are to respond in that moment, to sit on the comment and address it at a later time, or to totally ignore the exchange. The choice you make isn't really the issue at hand here.

The point is, whichever path you choose, do your best to move on once the decision is made. Do not perseverate and think about what you should have done or could have said. Make a decision, be OK with it, and move beyond that point. If, in retrospect, you would like to have handled the situation differently, then store it in the parking lot and respond with an alternate approach when a similar situation arises. But whatever you do, avoid losing energy over circumstances that shift your focus away from your purpose, goals, and time needed for others.

The Glue: Focus only on those things that keep you on course to achieving the goals set for your team, your organization, and yourself. Expand your capacity to learn from the decisions you make without losing too much energy over the outcome.

2. Avoid the "Everything to Everyone" Trap

With the menu of items you need to accomplish, you cannot afford to be everything to everyone. But let's face it—leaders often fall into this trap, and do so with great ease. There may be a variety of reasons we feel we should have all the answers and control all of the strings, but none of them are worth the price we end up paying.

You are only one person, and are part of a larger operating system. When you try to be everything to everyone, you're likely to set off a number of spiraling outcomes and events of which you are probably not even aware. As a simple example, you know that you cannot possibly have an answer to every question that a constituent poses. Too often, however, those in formal leadership positions don't want to appear unknowledgeable, so they stretch and flex to grind out an answer. What clearly happens in this case is that they give incomplete and inaccurate information that misguides or confuses the person asking the question.

There are other concerns leaders face when operating in this silo mentality. Making a habit of passing off less-than-sound information rapidly dilutes credibility, and has obvious long-term effects on ability to connect and relate to a constituency. As we will discuss later, operating in this manner also closes off channels for the development of others.

As this pitfall relates even more directly to energy, feeling the need to have all of the answers and to control all events is very consuming. Such self-imposed and unrealistic requirements suffocate your ability to be agile and respond to other issues that really do require your undivided attention.

The answer, then, is to shift lenses. Instead of seeing yourself as the end-all, begin to view yourself as a resource. Become comfortable with not knowing everything, and embrace the notion of being the "resource leader." Your constituents don't expect you to know everything, but they often do expect that you can aid them in getting their questions answered and needs met. That is, in fact, one of your key jobs as a leader.

The Glue: Shift from the mode of all-knowing to that of resource leader in order to better funnel your energy. Strengthen credibility through the demonstration of trustworthiness, and by exemplifying that you're a nimble thinker.

3. Plug Leaks

We all have weaknesses and we all have things that tend to minimize our impact as leaders. We often use the term "Achilles' heel" to describe soft spots in our personality or the situations that set us off. In order to be an effective leader, you must be able to plug energy leaks.

Therefore, it is critical that leaders understand where they lose energy before attempting to actually patch up or plug the leaks. A great place to begin is by going back to the first sticking point in this chapter. Where do you find yourself being overly concerned or overly consumed with issues that distract your focus from the tasks at hand? What individuals seem to set you off and take you away from your game plan every time you even hear their name? When do you repeatedly find yourself saying, "I should have said …" or "I wish I would have …"? These are just a few very simple yet common examples of how you can begin to identify where you might be losing energy.

Once you figure out where the leaks are occurring, it's time to take some bona fide action. You have to commit to some serious internal auditing at this juncture by monitoring your actions, reactions, and responses to daily interactions, especially in pressurized situations. Then it's time to choose some new and improved habits.

If you're aware of the fact that every time a particular employee asks you for clarification around a work function—whether they should know how to perform it independently or not—you become easily frustrated, then it's time to choose a new response. Granted, a legitimate competency issue may be resurfacing over and over with this employee, but that doesn't mean your reaction has to consistently parallel that flaw. Find a productive way of dealing with the employee's lagging competence, and a way of distancing your reaction to this deficiency. Then you're choosing to respond to a problem, as opposed to reacting to a behavior.

Within your role as a leader, this is also a tremendous opportunity to help your constituents become more focused, more decisive, and more positive about their work environment.

The Glue: Identify and plug energy leaks through regular self-monitoring. By doing so, you're better able to maintain focus, be more effective for issues that matter, and actually enjoy what you're doing.

4. Learn to Anticipate for Focus-Building

Learning to anticipate is a skill that has an unrealized cost-benefit of sorts—meaning, the time we put into the process might end up being all for naught in some cases, while in others, the time was worth its weight in gold.

The critical point here is that by learning and training ourselves to become better anticipators, we increase the probability that we're enhancing our efficiency, and more times than not, avoiding wasted energy. Even if you don't consider yourself to be much of a procrastinator, and taking action isn't a foreign concept in your playbook, this doesn't automatically translate to being able to anticipate for more strategic purposes.

Therefore, we have to learn how to strike a balance and understand how timing factors into the equation here. Similar to the envisioning process, learning how to anticipate with greater proficiency requires that we become better at planning. But before we can start planning, we have to slow ourselves down a bit and create the time and space to anticipate.

Chess players learn to anticipate. Now, I'm no star chess player, but I know that in order to be a fairly good player, you have to be able to think two, three, or even four steps ahead. In doing so, you're not only thinking about what will happen when you make your next move, but you'll start thinking about the move it will elicit from your competition. Then you're thinking about the move you're likely to make three or four steps down the line.

So what does becoming a better anticipator have to do with being a better leader? In leading a team or an organization, plenty. Most critically, the ability to anticipate is highly useful when realigning and refocusing as you move down the path to achieving vision. While the vision you craft for yourself, your team, or your organization may not shift dramatically in terms of the expected outcome, the path does, in fact, wind and shift. To achieve vision—any vision—we know that planning is a big part of the process. And we all know that ideas are only as successful as their execution.

Now, back to anticipation. As we establish our plans and strategies, thinking those two, three, or four steps ahead like the chess player helps us formulate the best possible moves as we progress down the path to our vision. Even if our anticipating efforts don't result in the outcome we had expected, the act of anticipating most likely saved us some energy and kept us better focused.

The Glue: Train yourself to become a more effective anticipator by taking the time to think like a chess player. Thinking two or three steps ahead can eliminate wasted energy, missteps, and deflated constituent morale due to foundationless and uninspiring plans.

5. Fill the Tank

Just as important as recognizing the difference between beneficial and detrimental energy expenditures, leaders will be better served, and will serve better, when they strike balance in a holistic sense. This means that you must approach life—not just your career—with a realization that balance is critical to your success, your health, and your performance as a leader.

Personal effectiveness—and, essentially, leadership effectiveness—requires that we replenish our fuel tank so that we can make an impact. In order to operate at peak performance in our daily functions, we must replenish our physical and mental expenditures. It's really no different than the car that needs refueling, or the athlete who requires rest periods in between intense workouts. In order to be an effective leader for the long haul, it's in your best interest to make this replenishment process a priority.

I know that carving out time for ourselves is easier said than done. So, then how do we apply this sticking point so that we can make a bona fide difference in our lives? The answer lies with a dose of reality, along with some creativity and desire.

In order to make this work, we have to willingly acknowledge that our work commitments, social calendars, civic commitments, and family responsibilities will present ebb and flow in demand levels. Along with that reality is the need to adjust the time we allocate to our personal replenishment periods. While we might not always be able to fit the ideal "tank-filling" activities into our schedule, there's usually the opportunity to downgrade or modify one of these activities. In doing so, we create a downshift in our mental and physical demands, and in turn fill the tank.

This presents an interesting paradox: while we're engaging in the tank-filling activities to maintain balance, it may seem at times that we're creating pressure and imbalances with other facets of our busy schedules. The key, then, is to identify activities that we know personally replenish the tank, commit to carving out time to integrate these activities into our leadership tank-filling agendas, and modify these activities when time gets tight.

The Glue: Leadership requires periods of mental and physical replenishment. Determine the activities that work for you, and then develop strategies to work them into your busy agenda, even in crunch times.

The Third Power:

Attitude

Highly effective leaders cultivate a powerful and sustained level of emotional fitness and hardiness.

The Foundation

Positive attitude alone is not enough. As a matter of fact, it's only the tip of the iceberg when we're talking about leadership effectiveness. But let's step back and think about this for a moment. When you think about a leader you've admired either in the past or currently, it is highly unlikely that he or she possessed a negative, or even toxic, attitude. Very few of us find inspiration in negative people, unless we're interested in being inspired toward negativity. There's little to derive from this negativity, and sustained following of such formally positioned leaders is highly unlikely.

When we refer to attitude within the construct of leadership development, we're not talking about false hope or leader-driven lip service. I'm also not suggesting that we should attempt to see the world through brightly tinted glasses, blocking out legitimate concerns and barriers. I am, however, implying that attitude is a key component of effective leadership. Further, there is an expectation that the leader will attempt to see the best in most situations, will look for the good in others, and will try at all costs to become part of the solution, and not the problem. Effective leadership requires that we adopt productive versus counterproductive behaviors, and doing so requires a steady effort.

It's about a cultivation process and the development of a strong and enduring mind-set. It involves intense perspective building. As an athlete conditions the body for a particular sport, so must a leader condition the mind. Training the mind is both relevant and critical for people interested in becoming effective leaders. In subscribing to the notion that people are naturally either positive or negative—hardwired with certain beliefs, and there's no changing the electrical board—some do choose to let mind-set development be a random process. However, if we agree that leadership development is a worthy and vital process, then we need to adopt "attitude" as a critical competency.

Kouzes and Posner (2002) cite studies about attitudinal differences in executives and how they handle stressful situations, referring to this capability as *psychological hardiness*. They describe this capability in terms of a willingness to engage in stressful events and take decisive action. Further, they highlight the critical fact that people won't follow leaders who aren't psychologically hardy or emotionally fit.

The ability to maintain a positive mind-set is often dependent upon a host of factors, which might range from the amount of pressure you're experiencing to the perception you hold of yourself or your capabilities. The significance of developing attitude and training the mind is to ensure that you consistently succeed, regardless of the circumstances you encounter. Remember, the demands you face when you're in a formal position of leadership are significant.

As previously mentioned, we in leadership positions have multiple constituents, and all require our attention and have expectations of us as their leaders. Developing a leader attitude is the ultimate linchpin for leadership success.

Attitude

Sticking Points

- Embody "Can-Do"

- Adopt a Best-Effort Standard

- Build Perspective

- Operate with Integrity

- Cultivate Agility

1. Embody "Can-Do"

Leaders have to believe. They offer strength and resolve when others simply want to pack up and give in. They uphold the vision so that others will see and stay on course. While these statements may sound a bit cliché, there's plenty of truth behind them. Think back again to those whom you admire for their leadership capabilities. The people you looked to for inspiration and direction are those who believe there is a great deal of possibility, even when times get really tough.

It's important to recognize that "can-do" is not an attempt to delude oneself or others. Being can-do is not cheerleading—it's choosing a productive mind-set that moves you and your team closer to where everyone wants to be. It's about looking at any situation, determining what has to be accomplished in order to get the job done, and then executing on the actions that need to be taken.

While every sticking point in the L5 model is applicable to everyone—regardless of whether or not you're a formal leader in an organization—can-do is a standout. When an individual demonstrates a productive mind-set and is solution oriented, they're going to attract people to themselves and their ideas. We've all observed this over and over in many aspects of our own lives. People that are can-do don't give up on their visions, their ideas, their goals, or their followers that easily. As a matter of fact, it takes a lot to derail can-do individuals. Regardless of where you currently see yourself on the often-vacillating continuums of leadership presence and self-confidence, you will take considerable strides if you simply appreciate the impact this tenet has on individual and team performance. The manner in which we approach any situation is absolutely embedded within our attitude arsenal. The challenge might be one of acting before thinking—falling into the trap of offering responses or taking actions that are counterproductive for ourselves, our team, and maybe even our organization. In practice, we see this most often with "change." Such knee-jerk reactions to change or newly imposed initiatives—of which we don't always have as much control as we'd like—tend to box-in our potential. We might very well be closing the door on new and interesting opportunities for learning, growth, and improvement.

When you're a formal leader, however, your attitude and mind-set take on an elevated degree of significance. Your constituents are always gauging your responses to everyday situations that arise, and are most certainly watching for your reactions to stressful and more volatile situations. These encounters are everyday diamonds in the rough—significant opportunities to make the difference in whether you and your team succeed or fall short of your expectations. This is where *not* setting the proper example is not an option. If your actions and attitude are counterproductive, you will be relying heavily on others to carry the team emotionally. In doing so, you run the inevitable risk of losing their faith and, eventually, their best effort.

The Glue: Bring out your best by choosing productive attitudes and eliminating counterproductive beliefs. Bring out the best in your team members by consistently demonstrating and reinforcing these productive behaviors.

2. Adopt a Best-Effort Standard

Life in and outside of the workplace offers twisting and winding roads. We think we've got everything figured out, and then, within the blink of an eye, things derail. This is a normal function of reality. Nonetheless, the intensity to which we derail has quite a bit to do with our state of emotional fitness or psychological hardiness.

Further, it's important to acknowledge that our capabilities to effectively lead will fluctuate. The premise of the L5 model, however, is that by raising awareness and cultivating the 5 Powers, we reduce the frequency and duration of derailing. "Best effort" is the best friend to "can-do." While we're training ourselves to approach everyday challenges with a productive and solution-oriented mind-set, we have to realize that this may look and feel a little different from day to day.

The effort you bring to your role as a leader is always your choice. If you find that you're repeatedly letting yourself down, then you need to ask some candid questions:

- Are you offering your best effort to those you lead?
- Are you setting your expectations so high that you're simply not allowing yourself to succeed?
- Are you expecting that it's never acceptable to fall short of the expectations you set for yourself, your team, or your organization?
- Are you being so critical of yourself that, no matter what you accomplish, it's never good enough?

These are just some of the questions you should be asking when you look in the mirror. Again, this sticking point is not intended to suggest that anything less than your best is ideal—nor is it suggesting that you should underachieve in your ventures and with your goals. It is clearly suggesting that "your best" may not be the same every day, and that not wasting time and energy on overanalyzing this reality is to your advantage.

As a leader, the effort you put forth sets the tone for the environment. Even though we each possess our own work ethic, motivation, and definition of success, constituents do expect that their leaders apply a reasonable degree of genuine effort.

The Glue: Apply your best effort with the realization that "your best" will vary. When evaluating the reasons for falling short of your expectations, be honest, realistic, forgiving, and willing to move on.

3. Build Perspective

Leaders have to make sense of situations, both for themselves and for the various stakeholder audiences. Therefore, we must learn how to become more responsive and less reactive in nature. Reactivity is usually more "after the fact," while responsiveness is arguably a more tempered and fluid approach to everyday experiences.

Perspective building requires that we check ourselves more frequently by once again slowing down our reactions to an event, verbal exchange, etc. This act of checking allows us to step back and figuratively remove ourselves from the event or circumstance just enough to look at things with a fresh set of eyes. This becomes an important skill for leaders at all levels of an organization, as reactionary behavior often leads to poor decision-making and missteps.

Increasing your perspective has many other benefits for your constituents, especially as it relates to the presence you project. As a leader, perspective-building venues are prime opportunities for you to model the same high-impact behavior that you want your constituents to demonstrate. If your initial reaction is to panic when a rapidly developing situation is unfolding, then your followers will most likely do the same. Similarly, if your initial reaction is to push back when change initiatives are introduced in your organization or business unit, then you may very well be demonstrating behaviors that constrict growth and limit potential for yourself, your team, and the organization as a whole—clearly, not the best method of modeling desired behaviors.

Even if constituents don't follow those who demonstrate less than productive leadership styles, they're missing out on the opportunity to build upon fertile ground as it relates to team and individual effectiveness. With that team-impact factor in mind, individuals and groups possess tremendous potential to develop exemplary products or services when they are able to gain perspective around their work relationships. All too often, however, teams fall into a black hole that is void of perspective and that affords no benefit of doubt. As individuals, we have so many opportunities to extend the benefit of doubt to each other when we're interacting in the workplace. The key is to build perspective so that we take the time to gather the necessary facts, consider the vast opportunities, and respect other's needs and motives.

As we condition ourselves to step back and build perspective, we're more likely to offer the benefit of doubt, and in so doing, will avoid closing off channels that might lead to a new way of accomplishing everyday objectives. On a larger and more dynamic scale of leadership, we're then demonstrating through action, not just our spoken words, that there are usually more options available than we acknowledge, especially when under pressure. It's the leader's job to construct a frame of sorts in order for the team to make sense of experiences before they reach the point of chaos.

This concept of perspective building reminds me of the gardens in China. Many are constructed with concrete walls that have seemingly strategic cutouts. This offers visitors a different view of the garden features with every new step along the garden path. With a new view at every turn, the hardscape and landscape seem to offer endless vantages.

The Glue: Make sense of everyday situations by creating perspective. Think of perspective building as a framework that allows you to see different angles and reach different solutions with greater clarity. Construct new windows for yourself and others so that opportunity is not self-limiting.

4. Operate with Integrity

When we think of integrity as a component of attitude, its place may not seem as overtly obvious. However, attitude by definition has to do with position or posture. This is highly relevant in that the positions you adopt and exercise around integrity have much to do with the degree of respect you'll earn and retain from constituents.

Operating in integrity means that there's a visible and even palpable thread of consistency between your beliefs, spoken words, and actions. While you may truly possess integrity as an individual, it often takes time and some degree of demonstrated competency to have a constituency fully appreciate your integrity level. Although this has always been the case with leadership, it is now most significant due to the vast number of high-profile leadership blunders witnessed in so many large corporations and organizations.

Therefore, with an ever-increasing importance on integrity, those in formal positions of management cannot afford to underestimate the impact that their words and actions have on others. Leaders need to be acutely aware of integrity levels, because once lost or tarnished, it's difficult to regain a constituency's confidence and trust.

There are a host of what might be classified as less blatant integrity breaches that are committed on a fairly regular basis. These are the situations in which you take actions or make comments that are in conflict with what you previously did or said. An example of this type of breach might be failing to provide the degree of support you promised a report prior to delegating a particular task. The extended outcome of such a breach is a future unwillingness of that same report to accept additional opportunities to stretch, and to accept more responsibility in general, due to fear of failure.

In some situations, this integrity breach may not even have been exposed to the masses, but it has been to you. These less obvious, but still damaging, breaches often surface in the form of a gut feeling that one experiences when an integrity issue arises. For example, a fellow manager negatively comments on another peer, only after that individual leaves the conference room—a simple example, but one many of us may be guilty of committing ourselves from time to time. In general, this comment seems harmless on the surface, but it's really an erosive behavior that serves no value to the betterment of the team or the organization at large. Further, over time these behaviors—especially if demonstrated by multiple parties and with more regularity—become deeply embedded in the culture of the organization itself. This simple example also extends out even further as it relates to trust. What individual around that same conference room table won't wonder whether he or she is being discussed when they leave the room?

Let's consider some reasons that leaders act without integrity:

- Fear or concern of being alienated by peers if they were to step up and take a stand or position that runs counter to others
- Discounting and rationalizing integrity infractions as being less significant than they truly are

- Convincing themselves that a minor infraction couldn't possibly transpire into, or lay the groundwork for, additional infractions

The key point here is that your integrity is always on the line as a leader. Your constituents are looking and listening for consistency between words and actions. You build long-term trust and solid team relations by demonstrating the courage to hold yourself and others responsible for the actions taken and words spoken.

Frequent introspection and elevated self-awareness is the only strategy a leader can apply to ensure that integrity is maintained in the greatest capacity.

The Glue: Never underestimate the force of your actions and spoken words on your constituents, as they watch and observe with great interest. Develop the courage required to hold yourself responsible for acting with integrity.

5. Cultivate Agility

A close cousin to building perspective is cultivating mental agility. As a matter of fact, it's when a leader possesses mental agility that he or she is able to gain and build this perspective. Effective leaders are nimble and flexible, fully realizing that change, in every sense of the word, is inevitable. There is little to no room in the leader's mental arsenal for a rigid, inflexible mind-set.

While cultivating agility is imperative for a number of reasons, we're going to focus here on the one most critical for leaders.

As we drive toward our visions, the Plan A we had in mind might no longer be a viable option. Some factor may have derailed the original plan, or we may have come to the conclusion on our own that a more productive plan is called for to reach our objectives. For that reason, conditioning yourself to "think big" and expanding your strategy playbook are imperative. In strategic planning development, we refer to this as a fallback strategy.

Learn to anticipate and envision a variety of outcomes. This is a worthwhile and productive process that may be performed independently or within the context of a team exercise. In either case, you're both developing and exercising the agility process.

Cultivating mental agility also has a great deal to do with our emotional maturity. When we're secure in our thoughts and beliefs, we're more open to others' perspectives. We not only tend to acknowledge the gray zones that exist in our everyday experiences, but we actively seek them out. We fully appreciate that there's greater opportunity for all involved.

When we are less secure in ourselves, we tend to contract. This leads to black-and-white thinking and self-limiting belief patterns. While this is counterproductive for any individual, there's a more detrimental effect when one is in a formal position of management. As we've noted over and over again, the decisions leaders make cascade onto others. When leaders operate with a constricted mind-set, they limit not only themselves, but also very often their teams and organizations.

The Glue: Condition yourself to seek out and become comfortable with the gray zones. As you move toward your visions, create Plan A, Plan B, and Plan C. Cultivating and possessing an agile mind-set propels the leader into a more dynamic realm.

The Fourth Power:

Relating

Highly effective leaders understand that genuinely relating to others is the underpinning of team success.

The Foundation

A leader's ability to relate to others is critical for many reasons. On the most basic of levels, constituents want to know that you ultimately care about them and hold their interests in mind. On more strategic and advanced levels, the manner and degree to which you are able to relate to your constituents will ultimately determine the success of the team and the organization. You cannot successfully communicate vision if you're unable to relate to your constituents. You will not be successful in developing others if you lack interest in relating to those same people.

Relating to others is usually one of the more prominent deficiencies among leaders in many industries and professions. For various reasons—such as the manner in which we were socialized throughout our formative years, our current maturity level, and our motives—those in formal positions of management sometimes fail to appreciate the need for genuine ability to connect to those they lead. Some additional reasons for this lack of connectivity may have a great deal to do with preconceived notions or deeply held beliefs about how managers and line employees are supposed to interact and coexist.

Leaders cannot afford to hold the belief that relating equates to weakness. Even professions and industries that have traditionally relied upon command-and-control styles of leadership have come to appreciate the fact that connecting to others is what allows teams, organizations, and even communities to succeed. Relating is not a sign of being a weak or insecure leader. Quite the opposite is true. Taking the time to relate to others by getting to know what's important to them, understanding their values, and listening to their personal visions is a sign of significant strength for a leader.

Even if you don't consider yourself to be a natural at relating to others, you can and must take some basic steps to ensure this competency is enhanced. Leaders who know how to effectively relate to their constituents lay fertile ground for a trustworthy and dynamic culture. Whether you've been leading for many years or are fairly new to the role, it's a fact that the people you lead expect a great deal from you. You're more likely to be afforded the benefit of the doubt in challenging times if you've previously taken the time to connect to others.

As you work toward evolving this power, be sure to measure your approach in an effort to avoid being perceived as patronizing or trite. Aim toward genuineness and avoid forced attempts at connecting to your team members. You're better served if you seize timely opportunities to build those relationships.

If relating to others is one of your strengths, then it's critical that you continue to evaluate the degree to which you are doing so successfully. Relationships are influenced by a number of issues, and are often impacted for reasons that may be well beyond your control or knowledge. Even with that said, ignoring this fact only increases the potential that disconnect is likely to become the norm as opposed to being the exception.

Relating

Sticking Points

- Be Visible

- Step Out of Your World

- Show Them You're Fallible

- Change Up Your Approach

- Share Successes

1. Be Visible

Visible leadership is not merely face time. As a matter of fact, the perception that you're offering up face time might be more damaging, since it feels and appears disingenuous. Sure, there are those who believe that simply getting in front of their constituents and making the rounds is the key, but most of us know differently. A leader's presence—be it physical, electronic or other—makes a statement to the constituency, and is just one of many factors that set the cultural tone for the team, business unit, board, or organization.

Being visible means genuinely connecting with the people. Depending upon the size of a team or organization, it might only be realistic for a leader to make contact with a small sector of people. Therefore, it truly comes down to the quality of your interactions, not the quantity. With today's ever-expanding technological advances, the opportunity to connect to others is greater than ever. Your visibility can be demonstrated through many avenues. And, quite frankly, this is a wise practice for building connectivity with constituents at all levels.

Timing also becomes a consideration with a leader's visibility. For example, a common mistake many leaders make is that they only increase their visibility when a crisis is on the rise, or when in the thick of an existing crisis. This bad habit sends a variety of messages to the constituency, none of which are positive. If you fail to consider this timing factor—regardless the size of your team—you might be sending any of the following messages:

- Your purpose is to be the heavy hand, the "bad guy," or the taskmaster.

  Outcome: People never get a chance to connect to or view you as a multidimensional figure, thereby limiting association from the more positive attributes of your role. In terms of organizational culture, this could induce and perpetuate unnecessary fear throughout the constituency, and result in having your messages lost in the delivery.

- The people working for and with you are only worthy of your time when problems exist.

  Outcome: People perceive that you view your position as more critical than theirs. Now while most would agree that some positions are more mission-critical for obvious reasons, everyone wants to feel that they're valued and respected on a very human level. Though this costs nothing, it is a principle that is often overlooked or forgotten by those in formal management positions.

- That regular and consistent communication is only important when in crisis mode.

  Outcome: Your constituents perceive these "limited time only" ramped up communication efforts as opportunities on management's behalf to rally support or even share blame for decisions over which they had little control.

While these are just a few examples, all are valid and happen every day in organizations of all sizes. One could argue that the term "management by walking around" has new and broader meaning today. There are so many innovative and effective strategies for connecting to your constituents today, so be creative. And never underestimate the value of being genuinely visible to all levels of constituents.

The Glue: Make visibility a best practice in your leadership arsenal. Maintaining a steady flow of open communication and connectivity in calmer times lessens fears that inhibit productivity and dialogue when—and not if—more challenging times are on the rise.

2. Step Out of Your World

Relating to others only happens when you're willing to take the necessary time to do so. As discussed in the previous sticking point, establishing communication and visibility is a necessity, and needs to be a very cognizant process. Stepping out of your own world means that you take time to understand others' perspectives, interests, goals, and dreams.

Even those leaders who are generally proficient at relating to others need to remind themselves to keep this sticking point on the front burner. It's very easy for emerging and seasoned leaders alike to get caught up in the complexities of their work responsibilities and let relationship-building take a backseat. We must be able to balance our docket and make time and room for others.

Relating to others doesn't require an inordinate amount of time and energy. In many instances, it simply means taking a few opportune and sincere moments to learn what's important to another individual, or to find out how a newly implemented change is impacting one's job. Again, you're trying to break down barriers and strengthen connections. To demonstrate how the power of connecting can literally change lives, I'll share a personal story that surprises me to this day.

One day about five years ago, I was having lunch at a restaurant. I noticed that the young woman taking my order seemed very distracted and a little under the emotional weather. Without wanting to seem too intrusive, I offered her a few minutes just to let her know that I noticed her state of distraction. I remember her telling me she had a lot going on, and that this was a difficult time in her life. To the best of my recollection, I offered no magic words or prophetic statements. I just remember taking a few minutes before my meal arrived to listen to her and offer some words of encouragement.

About two years later, some colleagues and I walked into another restaurant for lunch. As we were being seated, a woman approached me and said, "You're that motivation guy, aren't you?" When it was obvious to her that I did not recognize her, she said, "You came into another restaurant where I was working and talked to me one day. After we spoke, I went into drug rehab and have been clean ever since, and I just wanted to thank you." We exchanged a few more words, and I proceeded to sit down with my colleagues. They looked at me and said, "What did you say to her?" All I could do was recount my previous interaction and ponder what had happened.

The example above had nothing to do with money. I assure you it didn't require a significant investment in time. It had everything to do with a willingness to get out of my own world and connect to another person. The bottom line is this: willingness to get into another person's world can make a bigger difference than you'd ever imagine. Within the workplace, that small investment in the employees demonstrates that their world is as important as yours.

The Glue: When you take the time to step into another person's world, do so with zero expectation; you're not doing this for any self-gain or underlying agenda. If you do so with genuineness, the difference made can be invaluable, even if you never know the actual impact.

3. Show Them You're Fallible

Another black hole that we in formal positions of management can fall into is having difficulty admitting when we are wrong or don't know something. Strong and effective leaders know how to admit they've made a mistake without seeing this as a reflection on their personhood. Better yet, highly effective leaders know that it's only through recognizing mistakes and admitting when they don't have all the answers that they're able to realign, improve, and move on.

So what causes us to feel the need to contract and build up perceived walls of perfection when we're working with others? The answers are many, but for the sake of simplicity, let's just say that most of us possess the basic fear of "not knowing," and see it as the equivalent of incompetence. I suggest that aside from basic skills that you bring to any particular job, there's always more that you don't know than you do. It's when we are not willing to learn and grow that incompetence rears its head.

As a leader, when you demonstrate that making mistakes is an expected part of the creative process, you encourage people to use their minds more fully. You give people the green light to make suggestions and recommendations that might just lead to a new idea that changes a business practice for the better. Show your constituents through actions—not just words—that being resourceful is both how you learn and how you help others learn.

In order to master this sticking point, you have to check your ego at the door. You cannot fear how you will be perceived, or what people will think of you. It's not a sign of weakness to say "I don't know." It is a sign of weakness to say you know when in fact you really don't. Similarly, when you make a mistake, don't cover your tracks and avoid what's obvious to others. This leads to unnecessary speculation about you morals, motives, and true competence levels.

If as a leader you willingly and openly admit mistakes, you'll find that others might just be willing to step up and be more accountable.

Haven't we all said at one time or another "I wish he would be more accountable," or "I wish she would be more responsible"?

Why don't people assume greater accountability? Why aren't more people more responsible?

Although there is a plethora of reasons, I think it's reasonable to say that people might not want to be accountable due to fear. More specifically, people may be fearful of attaching themselves to the potential shortcomings, and fearful of the ramifications they might face. If this lack of accountability is more systemic within our organizations, the problem is obviously even greater. We then have cultures that miss critical opportunities to learn and grow. We also lose tremendous opportunity to reap the rewards of our efforts and ideas and, in essence, to experience our highest potential.

The Glue: Make a bona fide commitment to remove your ego from as many interactions as possible. When you don't know the answers or make a mistake, share it and learn from it. Refuse to struggle with the notion that mistakes are not in the leader's playbook. It's like struggling to hold sand in your palm: the tighter you grasp, the more grains fall to the ground.

4. Change Up Your Approach

As we better understand how to relate to others, it's helpful to appreciate that leaders can and should be able and willing to change up their approaches. This isn't to imply that we manipulate our personalities or compromise our integrity in an effort to connect to other people. It simply means that as leaders, our delivery and approach may need to be tailored to a specific situation, depending on the need of a constituent.

Most of us are now familiar with the terms *coaching* and *mentoring*. And while these two distinct modes of relating, developing and guiding are available to leaders they are often misunderstood and as a result, misused. There may be a number of reasons that any one manager chooses not to exercise these modes. However, it usually stems from a limited understanding of the mentoring or coaching process, or a general unwillingness to employ different approaches. The key is to utilize a variety of approaches to enhance your relationships with peers, direct reports and constituents at all levels. This also ensures that outcomes and objectives are more likely to be achieved.

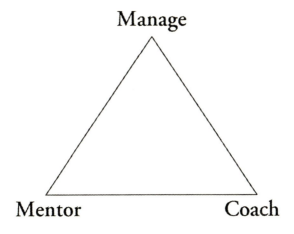

Manage

When you manage, you create structure and systems through which employees get things done. Your purpose in this mode is to make things happen through efficiency and effectiveness. This includes a host of functions ranging from project deadlines to performance management. Remember, your leadership skills impact just how effective you are in accomplishing any of these tactical and strategic responsibilities.

Mentor

When you mentor, you impart knowledge. It involves the teaching and sharing of information that one party has acquired over time, and the transfer of knowledge to another individual. It's best offered in a structured format, although some of the most successful experiences people have are the informal mentor relationships that evolve. A mentoring relationship might last a number of months or many years.

Coach

As a coach, you assume a unique and progressive role. Coaching is different from mentoring in that you're not really imparting a set of skills or book of knowledge. It differs from managing in that it's not about systems and structures. When you employ a coach approach, you're aiming to help someone get the best out of themselves, and doing so from their current base of strength. You're not focused on, and trying to eradicate, weaknesses; you're moving forward by asking key questions at just the right time, so that the individual being coached arrives at his own conclusions.

Of the three modes, coaching is truly an acquired skill. It requires a superb ability to relate and a very patient nature.

The Glue: Dispose of old ways of thinking about how mangers must behave. Relating is not a one-dimensional process, nor should your approach be one-dimensional. Effective leaders relate to others by possessing a high degree of sensitivity to timing, and then deploying the best approach.

5. Share Successes

Aside from integrity breaches, I don't know that there's any quicker way to lose the respect, confidence, and trust of a constituency than when a leader doesn't know how to, or doesn't care to, share in victories.

While I'll refrain from the "No I in team" speech, we cannot ignore the fact that emphasizing teamwork versus individual effort is in everyone's best interest. By all means, take credit where due. But also be careful to not minimize the efforts and roles that others play in the successes you experience. In more public forums, go out of your way to acknowledge these efforts, and thank people for their hard work and dedication.

As a leader, you should also be aware that part of your role is to recognize success in the first place. When constituents are caught up in their daily grind, they're not always looking for the smaller, but equally important, wins. Point out these occurrences, and explain how and why they're important. Explain how this progress is moving the team or the company closer to its vision and goals. Don't worry about the people to whom you report not being aware of your part in the outcome, be it a board of directors, a vice president, or a CEO. Good leaders have people around them that help them excel, and the people to whom you report will make the connection.

Take the opportunity to build *vertically*, and here's what I mean. Too often when we experience wins or positive outcomes, we see them as first-time events and unique in their occurrence. While this is certainly true some of the time, there are also many instances in which wins are interdependent. Further, the wins themselves can be built upon in an attempt to propel the next win. In this respect you can actually envision that you're building on these wins so that, instead of a horizontal trek, there's more of a vertical climb. When communicating with your team, create the imagery that forges this link.

Last, strive to make inclusion a standard in as many facets of your team and organization as possible. When leaders operate with this inclusion mentality, they open up the gates for people to be inspired and engaged. It's also helpful to recognize that inclusion—as it relates to sharing in future success—can occur within various capacities. I've heard some managers over the years voice the concern that including others to any significant capacity is an unadvisable practice, in that information may be misused or the intention misinterpreted. Most of us have also known of managers who limit knowledge sharing for purposes of self-gain or out of fear of losing their power.

Including constituents in matters such as decision-making and operational development will usually have a positive impact on morale because you are keeping people in the know. The key is to involve constituents to the degree that is appropriate for the particular initiative and at the particular point in time.

The Glue: Recognize and communicate wins of all degrees. While it's sometimes difficult to leave your ego to the side—especially when you've scored a grand slam—conditioning yourself to acknowledge the efforts of others has exponential benefits.

The Fifth Power:

Developing

Highly effective leaders embrace learning as an ongoing process, valuing it for themselves and for others.

The Foundation

While there is absolute interdependence between all of the powers in this model, each may also stand alone as an area of leadership competence and growth. As we prepare to discuss this fifth power, however, we must highlight its uniqueness, in that the scope of the development power spans the first four powers. In essence, the entire model is predicated on one of development.

The model suggests that you develop vision, focus, a leadership attitude, and relating capabilities. In the fifth power we not only discuss strategies for developing others in order to enhance their capabilities, but we also incorporate strategies for developing the leader from a life-balance approach.

A key point in this power is the relationship that exists between developing oneself and developing others. Quite simply, if you do not take the necessary time to develop yourself as a leader, it will become very challenging to develop other people. As a matter of fact, if you don't take the necessary time to develop yourself, you probably don't recognize or value its benefit in the first place. So we begin to see there's some irony, or paradox, that exists within the concept of development. With the time spent working on oneself to improve and become more effective, some might argue that there's too much focus on the individual and that the process seems somewhat egocentric. The counterargument to this perspective—the very core of the model—is that it's only when you do, in fact, take the necessary time to develop as an individual and as a leader that you're able to serve others to the degree that is both needed and appreciated. If we can embrace this belief, then we might begin to recognize just how important it becomes to take the time to develop.

Therefore, leaders should strive to make development, in its broadest sense, a best practice for themselves. You only achieve this when you continually look at the reflection in the pond, make an honest assessment of what you see, align your efforts, and then move into action.

Developing

Sticking Points

- Habituate Takeaways

- Create Endless Opportunity

- Master the Art of Delegation

- Create Balanced Development

- Exercise the 5 Powers

1. Habituate Takeaways

Developing has a lot to do with perspective-building, and one of our previously discussed glue ingredients plays a critical role here. Choice is the driver in that we either make the conscious decision to learn from situations, or we don't. If we choose to look at the proverbial glass as being half full versus half empty, then we can condition ourselves to always take something away from an encounter.

It is absolutely up to each and every individual to make the choice to learn. Leadership is about learning, and that learning needs to be ongoing. Just like leadership itself, the development process is dynamic, rather than linear and static. We, as leaders, however, need to continuously propel ourselves to learn and grow in order to stay fresh and bring our best to whatever it is we're aiming to accomplish.

We must adopt a mind-set around this sticking point. We should be capable of extracting learning opportunities from almost any situation, regardless of the outcome. The framework in which we operate, as related to definitions of success and failure, factors into the equation at this juncture. If we believe that opportunities to learn are everywhere, and that it's learning that leads to success, then we might argue that failure is only truly experienced when we choose not to learn from an experience. In this respect, we're never really failing, because we're choosing to walk away from a less-than-desirable outcome having learned something meaningful. Now I'm not suggesting this as a feel-good-at-all-costs strategy in which we delude ourselves. However, I am saying that we can weigh in heavier in the outcome of everyday experiences if we are willing to view these occurrences from a different perspective.

In terms of leading others, this is part of the job description. Leaders have to develop through example. You can explain how and why one needs to develop, but it requires something more; leaders have to seize the ample teaching moments that occur every day in which this principle can be reinforced through effective modeling.

The Glue: Condition yourself to extract takeaways from any experience you encounter, and coach others to do the same. Always ask yourself, "What can I learn from this situation?"

2. Create Endless Opportunity

Can you recall a time in your life when a door of opportunity just seemed to open up and you felt like the world was yours? You felt incredibly energized, like you received a power surge of sorts. You were elated, and probably even realized just how much potential your future held. When you've experienced these moments, you may have also wondered why these windows didn't seem to remain open for too long a period, or why they seemed to occur at such random. Building on the previous sticking point, the degree to which we develop and learn is up to us as individuals, and it doesn't have to be random. The fact is there's often considerable opportunity. We have to take the time to recognize the opportunity, and to appreciate the fact that it's sometimes about planting seeds and being patient while they take root.

There's little room for self-limiting behaviors in leadership. It's when leaders fall into this "small thinking" mode that constituents at all levels suffer.

In *Principle-Centered Leadership* (1992) Stephen Covey uses language and imagery that offer some context in how we view opportunity for ourselves as well as others. He describes scarcity and abundance as they relate to our mentalities and the beliefs we possess.

When we think about availability of resources—in any definition of the word—we can choose from two perspectives. In contrasting them, we'll use a pie as the metaphor for resources.

Perspective #1—scarcity mentality:

- The pie is only so big and cannot be enlarged. If we share a piece or pieces of the pie, there is that much less for us. Therefore, we opt to hold onto the pie for ourselves, and leave little or none for others.

Perspective #2—abundance mentality:

- The pie exists, but it is only limited in size by our belief system. We can choose to enlarge the pie, and offer some to others. As a matter of fact, when the boundaries are not self-imposed, we can continue to expand the pie. When we do so, not only do we personally not lose anything, we all gain.

The manner in which these perspectives relate to leadership and development is significant. When leaders adopt and apply an abundance mentality, they experience endless opportunity. Not fearing the progress of others, they are willing to share information freely and teach critical skills. Not fearing a loss of stature within their organization, they invest in others and relate at the most genuine of levels.

The Glue: Thinking big means thinking abundantly. Replace thoughts, language, and actions that constrict, constrain, and compromise development with thoughts, language, and actions that expand, enlarge, and harness development.

3. Master the Art of Delegation

There are so many reasons the process of delegation fails. The term itself has the potential to take on a not-so-flattering connotation, similar to that of empowerment. That said, both delegation and empowerment are necessary and beneficial processes in the realm of managing and leading, but it's the application of these processes that usually fails, not the concepts themselves.

Why do managers at all levels have considerable challenges with the delegation process? Here are just some of the reasons:

- We tell an employee that we're increasing her responsibility, but we don't effectively educate them with the necessary knowledge.

  Outcomes:
  * Inadequate completion of the task
  * Missed opportunity to teach for the long haul
  * Employee feels demoralized and incompetent
  * Employee lacks confidence for future stretch opportunities

- We don't make our expectations crystal-clear regarding timelines, outcomes, standards, etc., when issuing the request in the first place.

  Outcomes:
  * Manager experiences frustration with outcomes
  * The inadequacy of the final outcome hampers and impedes other functions of the team
  * Productivity is never up to reasonable standard
  * Employee is confused with the lack of direction

- We stop relying on certain team members when they underperform, and then add their workload to our task list or to that of other teammates.

  Outcome:
  * The employee never has the opportunity to realign his efforts and learn for the future
  * Team members become frustrated with each other, and begin to perceive inequity
  * Communication breaks down between team members, and work relationships erode
  * The manager perpetuates the substandard performance, and questions regarding his own credibility begin to surface

We can see with just these examples alone how delegation deficiencies can lead to a host of counterproductive and unwanted outcomes. Managers need to lead through skillful delegation for the betterment of all parties. When we don't refine these skills, we end up dumping versus delegating. When we don't refine these skills, we end up "reverse-delegating" in that we back out of the delegation process and, as previously mentioned, add to the existing workloads of higher-performing employees.

In order to ensure that we're delegating effectively, a good start would be to counter the reasons for ineffective delegation just noted. Here are some key strategies:

- Provide the opportunity for people to stretch and grow.

- Provide people with the proper training and education in order to successfully execute on these stretch experiences.
- Once you're confident that the training has translated into learning, step back and let people perform.
- Check in to ensure that people are succeeding, and determine if additional training is required.
- Evaluate your decisions around the delegation process, remaining sensitive to the fact that these decisions impact constituent morale, team relations, and performance in every dimension imaginable.

The Glue: Use delegation as a tool for development, not merely as a means of accomplishing to-do lists. Ensure that training is translating into learning so that efforts are sustainable and long term.

4. Create Balanced Development

Effective leaders are usually balanced individuals. As we've discussed all along, the amounts of energy required to lead others and ourselves is substantial. Think about this in the most basic of terms. As individuals we perform best when we're refreshed and recharged. Our thinking is crisper, and the decisions we make usually result in more positive outcomes. Recovery time for leadership development is no different and equally as imperative.

I suggest you refer to the personal development wheel included in this section, and either start thinking about or reinforce an existing standard with its use. The wheel is divided into various sections, referred to as dimensions. These dimensions are the areas in your life that mean something to you, and are part of what makes you the individual you are today. As you use the chart, create your own dimensions, and make the tool work best for you.

The purpose of the tool is to strive for some reasonable degree of balance between each of the dimensions at all times. Realistically speaking, complete balance is rare for extended durations. When work life gets even busier than usual, as when we're up against a deadline, something has to give in another one of our dimensions. When extra time is necessary on a given week with a volunteer organization with which you work, attention to your physical dimension might temporarily become deficient. The point is these imbalances will always exist to some degree. Acknowledging that this is rather common and normal for most of us is important, as is allocating necessary energy to the realignment and rebalancing of the dimensions in our wheel.

Once you've determined your dimensions, develop goals using the SMART process (i.e., specific, measurable, attainable, relevant, and time-bound). From that point, consider and plot out the action steps required to meet the goals you've established. Finally, consider the habits you'll need to develop in order to meet the goals and support the action steps. Revisit your plan regularly, and adjust as required.

The Glue: Strive to become a balanced individual so that you create the foundation required of a balanced leader. Be willing to courageously demonstrate to others that leadership and life are not one-dimensional. It's only when we are willing to take stock and recharge that we give our best to everyone with whom we come in contact. Our constituents at all levels deserve our best.

PERSONAL DEVELOPMENT WHEEL

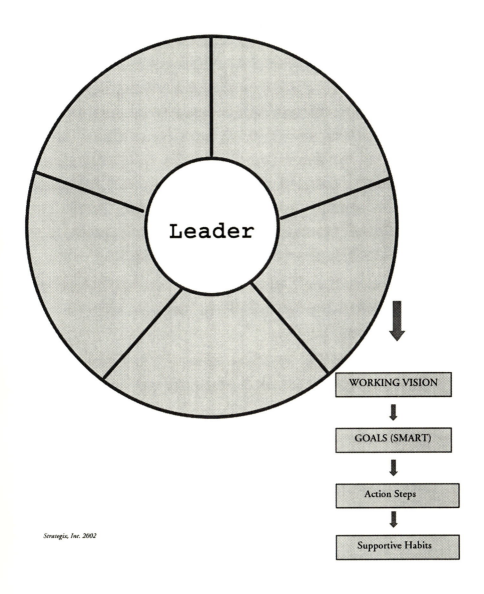

5. Exercise the 5 Powers

As we close out with the fifth power, and the last of the sticking points in the L5 model, let's create some context by weaving the material together and reinforcing key points of interest.

While the specific characteristics and traits that leaders need to possess could be debated decade upon decade on a scholarly level, I have outlined what I believe are the most critical for sustained growth. Wherever you fall on the leadership continuum—emerging, seasoned, etc.—cultivating the 5 Powers and applying the bonding agents will most certainly fortify your efforts and focus you on accelerating your development. Here are some highlights as you begin to apply the model:

- Continually identify your leadership capacity by checking the foundation points of vision, focus, attitude, relating, and developing.
- Always apply the bonding agent (G2), as choice and awareness are the drivers for personal and leadership success.
- Development is not static and linear. While the opportunity to build on past experiences is always available, shortcomings in your past are not predictors of your future.

The Glue: Use the L5 model as a framework for continuous growth and learning. As you venture on the path of leadership development, be confident knowing that it's only when you commit to serving yourself that you can commit to serving others.

LEADERSHIP IN ACTION

Clarity is the antidote to anxiety, and therefore clarity is the preoccupation of the effective leader. If you do nothing else as a leader, be clear.

—Marcus Buckingham

The following pages encompass scenarios that any leader, on any day of the week, may encounter. As you digest these scenarios, analyze how the characters integrate the powers in our model, and then ask yourself the following questions:

- Are they proficient at incorporating the principles?
- What might they have done differently?
- Did they exercise and apply the bonding agents?

Scenario One
The Script

Robert has just been hired into an organization at a midlevel management position. Prior to joining the organization, he held a similar position at a national competitor. Robert will be responsible for leading a division of seasoned employees, many of whom have their own ideas of how things should get done. His team is smart, efficient, and often viewed as the high producers within the company.

Robert comes to his new role with great enthusiasm and many ideas of his own. However, he's issued the gentle warning by his boss that he proceed with caution on change initiatives. She admits to Robert that he'll probably find a handful of issues that need to be addressed, but to take it slowly and not "ruffle too many feathers."

Now Robert is beginning to wonder if his predecessor faced these same challenges, and whether they were responsible for his exit after only seven months of service. Robert finds that he is dwelling on these thoughts, and then recognizes that he is drifting. He quickly gets himself together and decides that regardless his team's disposition and the admonition from his boss, he is here for the time being and is committed to making this new position work in everyone's favor.

After his second day on the job, Robert wants to move into action with a team meeting. His intentions for the meeting are to explain his style of leadership to the team, share his vision for the department, and set some ground rules.

As the meeting commences, Robert's confidence in the interaction increases. Some heads nod in agreement, and the flow seems relaxed for the most part. He tells them what he believes the strengths and weaknesses of the team are from his perspective. He then offers some timelines on changes he anticipates for the department. Throughout the meeting there is no actual dialogue among the team members. As he walks further down the path and talks about changes that he wants to see take place within the department, pushback begins to surface. The nods of approval come to a halt and the displeasure on their faces becomes quite visible. The conversation is now bidirectional, although not because Robert has requested their input. The exchange is even getting a little heated until Robert's boss—who is sitting in on the meeting—suggests they adjourn and table certain topics for the next meeting. With that, the conference room empties, with the exception of Robert and his boss. Robert admits rather sheepishly, "That wasn't such a banner start, was it?"

The Feedback

You're Robert's boss. You just witnessed a fairly significant meltdown, and you're wondering how your new manager and team can recover. What advice would you offer to Robert right now?

The Upside
- Robert is bringing enthusiasm to the position.
- He has ideas and is not afraid of driving change.

- He's willing to openly share his thoughts, even after his boss warned of some strong undercurrents in the form of subcultures.
- Robert has a high-performing team to work with, and they're proven within the organization.
- His boss appears supportive and willing to let him take the lead.
- Robert appears to have gotten some buy-in during the initial stages of the meeting.

The Challenge
- Robert has taken a few steps back with the team, and he may have lost some credibility.
- Robert's ego may be a bit bruised.
- Issues have been opened that aren't anywhere near resolution.
- His boss may be wondering why Robert didn't heed her advice about suggesting change so early in the game.
- Robert's ability to create connectivity with his team may be a bit strained at this juncture.

Rewind and Take Two
Here are some considerations for how Robert may have handled the situation differently:
- Robert's inaugural meeting should have been more exploratory. He probably doesn't really know enough to make bold statements about strengths and weaknesses of

the team. He would have been better served by informing his team that this is an area of discovery and focus for himself as the new manager. Further, he could explain that he'd like to garner their feedback over the coming weeks as he continues to formulate his perspectives.

- Robert hasn't had the necessary time to form even the most basic of relationships with his team members. Instead of setting ground rules and explaining his leadership style, he could have simply explained his background and his interest and excitement in working with this team. He may have also used the forum to genuinely recognize the accomplishments that his boss noted. This was an opportunity to acknowledge the team's high-performance history within the company. This would demonstrate that he cared enough to do his homework and that past performance was important and noteworthy.

- While one of Robert's true strengths is his enthusiasm, tempering it a bit might have been advisable with regard to his vision. He could have shared a glimpse of his vision with the team while, at the same time, articulating that it was preliminary and evolving at this juncture. He probably required more time in his role to set a vision for the team. Robert also may have missed a key principle in vision development in that he had an opportunity to work on building a shared vision by including the team in the process. While it is important for leaders to craft and communicate their vision, including others in the process and eliciting their visions is beneficial and often preferable.

Bona fide buy-in is much easier when constituents are part of the process.

- Robert could have downshifted the tone of the meeting when he realized the direction it was going. He could have simply informed the team that he probably was moving too fast, and that the topics on the table required more time than was available. In this regard, he wouldn't have needed his boss to step in as the equalizer of sorts. It would have also demonstrated that he was capable of "reverse gearing" and skillful redirection.

Where Does Robert Go from Here?

Here is what we might suggest to someone in Robert's situation:

- Step one is to do some damage control by creating a foundation for successful team interaction.
- Call a meeting for the following week, and have an agenda that includes topics generated by all parties involved.
- Open the meeting with a recap of the last meeting's less-than-favorable conclusion. Stepping over this issue as if it never occurred would be a mistake. Acknowledge the occurrence in public, and then move beyond it. You are not apologizing for the event; you're simply recognizing that things didn't go as planned, and that you'd like to have a stronger start.
- While you want to focus the team on smaller-picture items at the next meeting, you should be willing to entertain preliminary strategic discussion if generated by a team member.

- Inform the team there will be time in subsequent meetings to address the more complex issues.
- Set up one-on-one meeting times with each member in order to learn more about them with respect to their strengths, areas of developmental interest, and vision. Find out what's important to each of the team members, and ask what makes them most proud of the team. You can use this time to clarify your expectations, but it's more about them, and not you, at this juncture.
- Inform the person to whom you report of your plans. They're now aware of the challenges you're facing, so it's important for them to understand how you intend to address the issues at hand. This gives them an opportunity to weigh in and offer some insight.
- Take stock of your leadership capacity. You're in this position because you're capable and talented. Rely on the skills that got you where you are, but keep looking for that reflection in the pond.
- Don't worry so much about explaining your style of leadership in words, as this is often perceived as self-serving. Rather, demonstrate your style through your actions by raising your awareness level.

Scenario Two
The Script

Alex is being considered for a vice-president position of a company in the mid-stages of its business cycle. The position is newly created in that it's the first time a senior manager will be overseeing this particular division. The company has a small executive team, and a small group of investors who like to know what's going on with the business. Alex comes to the organization with about eight years of supervisory and management experience.

The other senior managers are very impressed with Alex during his interviews, and the CEO is immediately enamored with his drive and innovative ideas. He views this as an opportunity to infuse some fresh blood into the team and add a spark. Prior to his being hired, there is one manager who has some reservations about Alex. You see, it has come to the senior management team's attention that while Alex has an impressive work history, some questions were raised upon completing the pre-hire reference checks with respect to his drive and the price others sometimes paid to achieve his business objectives.

In a private conversation, this particular manager remains firm in his concerns. He urges the CEO to take some time and think this decision over a bit before acting. The manager emphasizes that the reason the company is so successful has everything to do with the deep respect the team members hold for each other and culture they've created as a complimentary team.

While the CEO appears to appreciate the manager's perspective, his mind is clearly set on the hire. The CEO wants a new superstar, so the decision is final.

Over the course of the first month, Alex appears to work fairly well within the executive team. During meetings, he always adds his perspective and is usually open minded toward his team members. His demeanor is a little edgy—however, nothing the team and the CEO aren't accustomed to in reasonable doses. Although this is a part of the creative tension that the team relishes, Alex raises a few eyebrows.

About this same time, some rumbling below the surface is starting to occur, according to some midlevel managers who report to Alex. Both Alex's peers and the CEO are getting feedback that his sometimes bull-like approach is beginning to concern people, and carnage is about to show up in his wake. The CEO is now convinced that he should have listened to the warnings, and decides to counsel Alex before this goes too far.

When the meeting commences, the conversation is delivered in a caring but direct manner. The CEO wants to ensure that Alex is clear about relating better to others and that Alex is both willing and able to support the culture that is so valued throughout the organization. To the CEO's surprise, Alex looks him straight in the eye and thanks him for his candor. Alex also indicates that he is never quite sure how others receive his approach. He also states that he doesn't want his performance or constituents to suffer due to poor leadership.

In order to support his development, the CEO assigns another senior manager to be Alex's formal mentor, and even hires an executive coach to work with him on leadership development. From that point on, Alex demonstrates significant improvement in his ability to lead. He slips into some old habits now and then, but this is now the exception rather than the rule.

The Feedback

You're an organizational development consultant observing the scenario that just unfolded. What suggestions might you offer as to what went well and how like matters could be handled in the future?

What went well in this scenario?

- The executive team had a member that was willing to speak up, and who did so for what appeared to be the right reasons.
- The CEO moved into quick action to address the performance issues once he realized that the issues might have been more systemic in nature.
- The CEO was willing to support the new VP in his development as a leader by assigning a mentor and securing an executive coach.
- Alex was able to realign his behaviors once the leadership challenges were brought to his attention.
- Alex was actually appreciative that someone had the courage to talk to him openly about the challenges.

How might similar matters be handled in the future?
- Additional dialogue among the executive team would have been prudent, especially once a concern by a team member was communicated. While every position in an organization is important, this newly developed senior position required critical analysis. Each member of the team should possess a reasonable understanding of the role and the associated responsibilities.
- While the plan to assign a mentor was wise and proved to be of benefit in the long run, doing so even earlier may have exposed some of the challenges and accelerated the alignment process. In order to ensure individual, team, and organizational success, early development planning is in everyone's best interest. The use of both mentors and coaches is valuable at any stage in development, but it's very helpful to consider timing. If the decision to assign or retain a coach or mentor is only exercised when performance or leadership issues surface, then the effort is more remedial in nature. It's prudent and more effective to tackle the development process proactively, using coaching or mentoring as a form of acceleration versus remediation.

Overall Analysis

More went well in this particular scenario than might have been expected. However, I wanted to highlight the aspect of urgency. The key was the CEO's responsiveness to the feedback he was receiving and his willingness to preserve this aspect of his organization's culture. All too often managers at all levels step over the early warning signs that someone needs guidance or help. Be it due to time, energy, willingness, or even the courage to tell someone what they might not want to hear, this form of avoidance almost always leads to counterproductive and negative outcomes.

We also have Alex to thank. He was willing to listen to and accept the feedback. This is not always so easy, regardless of our level of education and technical training. Then, along with some additional resources and feedback, Alex was able to realign his leadership behaviors. What's important is that he was beginning to experience some key shifts in perspective and then changing the way he got things done. Now, along with his personal success, he was equally interested in team and organizational success.

LEADERSHIP CAPACITY: *MEASURING YOUR SUCCESS*

Leadership Capacity (LC) is the term we use to define your ability to lead with effectiveness and impact. Keep in mind that, as we've said before, LC is not static. Your ability to lead with impact is challenged on a regular basis. There will be any multitude of factors that can derail your focus, challenge your beliefs, and make you question just how well you're doing as a leader. I have been in the presence of many a leader in various industries who, when under dramatic pressure, begins to question his or her ability to lead. It's critical for a leader to be able to work through these challenging experiences and recognize them for what they are.

These moments are learning experiences in the making that help mold you as a leader. Do they define you as a leader? Maybe, and maybe not. In some constituents' eyes, their definition of your leadership will come down to one experience, one moment in time. Others will recognize you for who you are, and not strictly for single moments in time. In the grand scheme, it's also refreshing to know that capacity fluctuates, and that your past is not necessarily a final blueprint of your future success as a leader.

Through this process of development, we will see that LC is measurable and can be used as an indicator of our capacity at any point in time. So why is this relevant to leaders, and why should we be interested in, or concerned with, being able to measure this capacity? Quite simply, when we apply a value or rating to our capacity to lead, we bring our readiness to the surface. In doing so, we can then realign our focus with greater awareness and ease.

Here's the formula on which the L5 model is based:

$$L5 + G2 = LC$$

This means that the degree to which each of the 5 Powers is developed, plus the application of the two bonding agents (choice and awareness), equals your ability to lead at any time. More specifically, the higher the LC rating, the greater quality and impact with which you will lead.

Driving Leadership Capacity (LC)

Refer to the following sticking points as a guide to develop your leadership capacity. Regularly assess how you are measuring up with any of these tenets. Then align and realign your efforts as often as needed to create a leadership development plan and establish goals for your development. Use the 5th Power Leadership Development Tool for this process.

Vision

Carve out time to make visioning a practice. Shift from random to intentional envisioning.

Communicate your vision with conviction and clarity. Take stock of your "stakeholder Rolodex."

Use vision to create a clear picture of desired future states, reduce fear of the unknown, and inspire others to greater heights.

Vision-driven change requires some degree of urgency in order to engage people and move them into action. Providing psychological safety shows them you care about their stake in that change.

Increase awareness around your personal beliefs and values so that you better understand your responses and level of leadership effectiveness.

Focus

Focus only on those things that keep you on course to achieving the goals set for your team, your organization, and yourself. Expand your capacity to learn from the decisions you make without losing too much energy over the outcome.

Shift from the mode of all-knowing to that of resource leader in order to better funnel your energy. Strengthen credibility through the demonstration of trustworthiness, and by exemplifying that you're a nimble thinker.

Identify and plug energy leaks through regular self-monitoring. By doing so, you're better able to maintain focus, be more effective for issues that matter, and actually enjoy what you're doing.

Train yourself to become a more effective anticipator by taking the time to think like a chess player. Thinking two or three steps ahead can eliminate wasted energy, missteps, and deflated constituent morale due to foundationless and uninspiring plans.

Leadership requires periods of mental and physical replenishment. Determine the activities that work for you, and then develop strategies to work them into your busy agenda, even in crunch times.

Attitude

Bring out your best by choosing productive attitudes and eliminating counterproductive beliefs. Bring out the best in your team members by consistently demonstrating and reinforcing these productive behaviors.

Apply your best effort with the realization that your best will vary. When evaluating the reasons for falling short of your expectations, be honest, realistic, forgiving, and willing to move on.

Make sense of everyday situations by creating perspective. Think of perspective-building as a framework that allows you to see different angles and reach different solutions with greater clarity. Construct new windows for yourself and others so that opportunity is not self-limiting.

Never underestimate the force of your actions and spoken words on your constituents, as they watch and observe with great interest. Develop the courage required to hold yourself responsible for acting with integrity.

Condition yourself to seek out and become comfortable with the gray zones. As you move toward your visions, create Plan A, Plan B, and Plan C. Cultivating and possessing an agile mind-set propels the leader into a more dynamic realm.

Relating

Make visibility a best practice in your leadership arsenal. Maintaining a steady flow of open communication and connectivity in calmer times lessens fears that inhibit productivity and dialogue when—and not if—more challenging times are on the rise.

When you take the time to step into another person's world, do so with zero expectation; you're not doing this for any self-gain or underlying agenda. If you do so with genuineness, the difference made can be invaluable, even if you never know the actual impact.

Make a bona fide commitment to extract your ego out of as many interactions as possible. When you don't know the answers, or make a mistake, share it and learn from it. Refuse to struggle with the notion that mistakes are not in the leader's playbook. It's like struggling to hold sand in your palm—the tighter you grasp, the more grains fall to the ground.

Dispose of old ways of thinking about how mangers must behave. Relating is not a one-dimensional process, nor should your approach be one-dimensional. Effective leaders relate to others by possessing a high degree of sensitivity to timing, and then deploying the best approach.

Recognize and communicate wins of all degrees. While it's sometimes difficult to leave your ego to the side—

especially when you've scored a grand slam—conditioning yourself to acknowledge the efforts of others has exponential benefits.

Developing

Condition yourself to extract takeaways from any experience you encounter, and coach others to do the same. Always ask yourself, "What can I learn from this situation?"

Thinking big means thinking abundantly. Replace thoughts, language, and actions that constrict, constrain, and compromise development with thoughts, language, and actions that expand, enlarge, and harness development.

Use delegation as a tool for development, not merely as a means of accomplishing to-do lists. Ensure that training is translating into learning so that efforts are sustainable and long term.

Strive to become a balanced individual so that you create the foundation required of a balanced leader. Be willing to courageously demonstrate to others that leadership and life are not one-dimensional. It's only when we are willing to take stock and recharge that we give our best to everyone with whom we come in contact. Our constituents at all levels deserve our best.

Use the L5 model as a framework for continuous growth and learning. As you venture on the path of leadership development, be confident knowing that it's only when you commit to serving yourself that you can commit to serving others.

CONCLUSION

Your skills and competency as a leader will be challenged—that is the simple and sometimes difficult truth. Such challenges might arise from any number of circumstances—from rapid shifts in business strategy that create more tumultuous times to clearly articulating vision in your everyday leadership role in seemingly less turbulent times. In either of these scenarios, or anywhere in between on the leadership scale of challenges, offering your best can be the difference between marginal and outstanding team and organizational performance.

The 5 Powers, the twenty-five sticking points, and the accompanying 5th Power Leadership Development Tool are designed as a blueprint for leaders to gauge and accelerate capacity. While the concepts and tool offer a serious yet practical framework, it's important to note that change requires action. It's not enough to gauge your leadership capacity if you're not willing to set meaningful goals to improve the identified areas of development. Similarly, it's not enough to establish goals for yourself that are intended to improve the quality in which you show up as a leader if you're not sincere about making shifts through taking action.

When we dust off the confusion about what leadership is and what it is not, and remove the sometimes-existing fear of stepping up to lead with a sense of conviction, we begin to see and feel the impact that well-executed leadership can have on any and every aspect of our lives. We begin to take calculated chances, because we're not afraid to experience less-than-perfect results. We become interested in genuinely connecting with others so that the "What's in it for me?" exists closer to the surface. We communicate our visions more vividly because we've taken the time to envision a future state. The bottom line is that developing into a more effective leader pays off, and it does so for all with whom you come into contact.

As you learn to apply the tenets from the model and utilize the 5th Power tool, I'd like to leave you with some closing thoughts about leadership and why embarking on this path is both a necessary and worthwhile venture:

- Leadership should not be thought of as a function that is limited or exclusive to specific industries or professions—any organization or team needs good leaders in order to reach its potential.

- Accelerating your leadership capacity allows you to experience greater satisfaction in everything you do, because opportunities for leadership happen everywhere.

- Reminding yourself of the dynamic nature of leadership development is helpful since you will encounter variables that redirect efforts and act upon your capabilities.

- Effective leadership is the answer to so many of the challenges that we experience in our daily lives. It is truly empowering when we recognize that it has been, and always will be, a question of choice in wanting to make a difference, and that we possess the capability to make changes.

APPENDIX A

DRIVING LEADERSHIP CAPACITY— POCKET VERSION

Vision

- Carve out time to make visioning a practice. Shift from random to intentional envisioning.
- Communicate your vision with conviction and clarity. Take stock of your "stakeholder Rolodex."
- Use vision to create a clear picture of desired future states, reduce fear of the unknown, and inspire others to greater heights.
- Vision-driven change requires some degree of urgency in order to engage people and move them into action. Providing psychological safety shows them you care about their stake in that change.
- Increase awareness around your personal beliefs and values so that you better understand your responses and level of leadership effectiveness.

Focus

- Focus only on those things that keep you on course to achieving the goals set for your team, your organization, and yourself. Expand your capacity to learn from the decisions you make without losing too much energy over the outcome.

- Shift from the mode of all-knowing to that of resource leader in order to better funnel your energy. Strengthen credibility through the demonstration of trustworthiness, and by exemplifying that you're a nimble thinker.
- Identify and plug energy leaks through regular self-monitoring. By doing so, you're better able to maintain focus, be more effective for issues that matter, and actually enjoy what you're doing.
- Train yourself to become a more effective anticipator by taking the time to think like a chess player. Thinking two or three steps ahead can eliminate wasted energy, missteps, and deflated constituent morale due to foundationless and uninspiring plans.
- Leadership requires periods of mental and physical replenishment. Determine the activities that work for you, and then develop strategies to work them into your busy agenda, even in crunch times.

Attitude

- Bring out your best by choosing productive attitudes and eliminating counterproductive beliefs. Bring out the best in your team members by consistently demonstrating and reinforcing these productive behaviors.

- Apply your best effort with the realization that your best will vary. When evaluating the reasons for falling short of your expectations, be honest, realistic, forgiving, and willing to move on.
- Make sense of everyday situations by creating perspective. Think of perspective-building as a framework that allows you to see different angles and reach different solutions with greater clarity. Construct new windows for yourself and others so that opportunity is not self-limiting.
- Never underestimate the force of your actions and spoken words on your constituents, as they watch and observe with great interest. Develop the courage required to hold yourself responsible for acting with integrity.
- Condition yourself to seek out and become comfortable with the gray zones. As you move toward your visions, create Plan A, Plan B, and Plan C. Cultivating and possessing an agile mind-set propels the leader into a more dynamic realm.

Relating

- Make visibility a best practice in your leadership arsenal. Maintaining a steady flow of open communication and connectivity in calmer times lessens fears that inhibit productivity and dialogue when—and not if—more challenging times are on the rise.
- When you take the time to step into another person's world, do so with zero expectation; you're not doing this for any self-gain or underlying agenda. If you do so with

genuineness, the difference made can be invaluable, even if you never know the actual impact.

- Make a bona fide commitment to extract your ego out of as many interactions as possible. When you don't know the answers or make a mistake, share it and learn from it. Refuse to struggle with the notion that mistakes are not in the leader's playbook. It's like struggling to hold sand in your palm—the tighter you grasp, the more grains fall to the ground.
- Dispose of old ways of thinking about how mangers must behave. Relating is not a one-dimensional process, nor should your approach be one-dimensional. Effective leaders relate to others by possessing a high degree of sensitivity to timing, and then deploying the best approach.
- Recognize and communicate wins of all degrees. While it's sometimes difficult to leave your ego to the side—especially when you've scored a grand slam—conditioning yourself to acknowledge the efforts of others has exponential benefits.

Developing

- Condition yourself to extract takeaways from any experience you encounter, and coach others to do the same. Always ask yourself, "What can I learn from this situation?"
- Thinking big means thinking abundantly. Replace thoughts, language, and actions that constrict, constrain, and compromise development with thoughts,

language, and actions that expand, enlarge, and harness development.

- Use delegation as a tool for development—not merely as a means of accomplishing to-do lists. Ensure that training is translating into learning so that efforts are sustainable and long term.
- Strive to become a balanced individual so you create the foundation required of a balanced leader. Be willing to courageously demonstrate to others that leadership and life are not one-dimensional. It's only when we are willing to take stock and recharge that we give our best to everyone with whom we come in contact. Our constituents at all levels deserve our best.
- Use the L5 model as a framework for continuous growth and learning. As you venture on the path of leadership development, be confident knowing that it's only when you commit to serving yourself that you can commit to serving others.

APPENDIX B

THE 5TH POWER

Leadership Development Tool©

Introduction

This tool has been designed for those in leadership roles at all levels and within all capacities. Its purpose is to identify key areas of development for the leader, and is grounded in the belief that leadership development is a continuous competency. A balanced leader will experience greater success in every aspect of both personal and professional life.

The 5th Power is divided into five sections that mirror the powers in the L5 model. Each section is composed of tenets derived from the sticking points. It is suggested that the tool be utilized on an ongoing basis. The objective is to increase the number of points accumulated in each of the powers.

If you are working with a professional coach, this tool is a valuable springboard for goal setting and action planning.

The 5th Power
Leadership Development Tool©

Instructions for Use

1. Complete each section of the tool in its entirety. Be very honest with your self-assessment, and give yourself the score that accurately reflects how you believe you are performing for any one of the powers. Each tenet may be awarded zero to four points, for a total of twenty possible points per power. A perfect score for the tool would be 100 points. Write the number you're assigning on the line to the right of each tenet. Place a check mark in the box to the left of the tenets that you want to designate as areas of focus for your leadership plan.

Scale:

1 = Rarely   2 = Occasionally   3 = Fairly Often
4 = Very Frequently

2. Add the totals at the bottom of each section. You may also then indicate your score using the Leadership Capacity (LC) Scorecard to gauge ongoing progress.

3. Based upon your scores and the powers you want to develop, begin the goal-setting process. Write goals with objectivity, and timelines for achievement. Use the SMART goal-setting standard. Also consider the action steps and supportive habits required to meet your goals.

4. Update and add goals as often as you see fit.

5. Update your leadership capacity points at least once per month to maintain focus on your leadership plan.

6. Be sure to make ample copies of the tool and its components.

The First Power: Vision

Whether you are leading a small work team or a large organization, having a strong sense of purpose and direction is key to your success.

☐ I set aside time to cultivate the envisioning process so that vision development is more intentional. _____

☐ I communicate vision with conviction and clarity to my various stakeholders. _____

☐ I create vivid images of my vision to inspire others. _____

☐ I strike a balance between communicating vision with a sense of urgency and acknowledging other's need for time to embrace the vision. _____

☐ I reflect upon my personal values and beliefs in order to better understand my direction and leadership decisions. _____

Total Vision Score _____

The Second Power: Focus

Effective leaders focus their energy and use it wisely. The leadership arena is demanding, and requires that you understand how to both conserve and expend energy.

☐ I apply my time and energy to those things that have the greatest impact on vision, goals, and things that make a difference. _____

☐ I build credibility and trust by serving as a resourceful leader. _____

☐ I plug energy leaks regularly so that I am at my best and maintaining focus. _____

☐ I am proficient at the skill of anticipating, and try to think three steps ahead. _____

☐ I integrate activities into my schedule that recharge me and replenish my energy. _____

Total Focus Score _____

The Third Power: Attitude

Leadership doesn't merely require a positive attitude. It's about cultivating a deep foundation of psychological fitness, and building perspective around both simple and complex everyday situations.

☐ I choose productive attitudes, believe in possibility and strive to avoid counterproductive behaviors. _____

☐ I consistently apply my best effort, fully acknowledging that my best effort will vary from time to time. _____

☐ I build perspective by responding more and reacting less. _____

☐ I demonstrate integrity through consistency in my words and actions. _____

☐ I am agile in my thoughts and am comfortable both seeking out and operating within these gray zones. _____

Total Attitude Score _____

The Fourth Power: Relating

Relating to constituents requires that leaders actually care about others. It can also be a delicate balancing act between leader visibility and genuine connectivity.

☐ I make visibility a best practice with constituents, and do so when the waters are calm as well as during more turbulent times. _____

☐ I seize opportunities to connect with others in a genuine manner, and not merely for self-gain. _____

☐ I am comfortable letting others know when I've made a mistake, and take the opportunity to teach them that making mistakes is not a weakness. _____

☐ I rely on a variety of relating approaches when interacting with constituents. _____

☐ I recognize and communicate efforts and wins of all degrees. _____

Total Relating Score _____

The Fifth Power: Developing

Leadership is an ongoing journey that entails broad-based learning for both leaders and their constituents.

☐ I see learning opportunities in almost any situation, and extract takeaways. _____

☐ I possess a mentality in which I see things as being abundant versus scarce. _____

☐ I delegate by teaching, letting go, and supporting, so that I ensure training translates into learning. _____

☐ I am a multidimensional leader in that I identify various aspects of my personhood and exercise balance between these dimensions. _____

☐ I strive to cultivate the 5 Powers by recognizing that choice and awareness drive and bind the powers. _____

Total Developing Score _____

Leadership Capacity Scorecard

Use this document to list your leadership capacity scores. As you retake the fifth power, refer back to these scores and compare your progress.

Date:
Scores: Vision _____ Focus _____ Attitude _____
Relating _____ Developing _____
                      Total Score/Leadership Capacity _____

Date:
Scores: Vision _____ Focus _____ Attitude _____
Relating _____ Developing _____
                      Total Score/Leadership Capacity _____

Date:
Scores: Vision _____ Focus _____ Attitude _____
Relating _____ Developing _____
                      Total Score/Leadership Capacity _____

Date:
Scores: Vision _____ Focus _____ Attitude _____
Relating _____ Developing _____
                      Total Score/Leadership Capacity _____

Date:
Scores: Vision _____ Focus _____ Attitude _____
Relating _____ Developing _____
                      Total Score/Leadership Capacity _____

The 5th Power
Leadership Development Tool©

Development Plan

Use this document to begin charting your goals based upon the results of your scorecard and the areas you want to develop.

Date:
Power:
Goal(s):

Action Step(s)/Supportive Habits:

Date:
Power:
Goal(s):

Action Step(s)/Supportive Habits:

Date:
Power:
Goal(s):

Action Step(s)/Supportive Habits:

REFERENCES

Cooper, R., and A. Sawaf. *Executive EQ: Emotional Intelligence in Leadership and Organizations.* New York: Perigee, 1997.

Covey, S. *Principle-Centered Leadership.* New York: Fireside, 1992.

Kouzes, J., and B. Posner. *The Leadership Challenge.* San Francisco: Jossey-Bass, 2002.

Kotter, J. *Leading Change.* Boston: Harvard Business School Press, 1996.

Schein, E. *Organizational Culture and Leadership.* San Francisco: Jossey-Bass, 1992.

For Information About:

• Leadership and Executive Coaching

• Leadership Development Planning

• Strategic Communication/Planning

• Speaking Engagements

Visit us at www.strategixleadership.com

INDEX
Page numbers in italic refer to images.

abundance mentality, 89
accountability, 76
actions, demonstrating leadership, 59
adversity, 8
agility, cultivating, 64
anticipation, 46
approaches, to leadership development, 6–7
attitude, 50, 115, 122–123
   definition of, 51
   sticking points, 53
   tenets, 131–132
awareness, 12, 15

balance, 93–94, 117
best effort, 56–57, 115

"can-do," 54
capacity, 111–112
challenges, to leadership, 119
China, gardens of, 59
choice, 12, 13–14
coaching, 77, 78–79
communicating, vision, 28–29
concerns, about leadership, 6
conditioning, 51–52
connection, and visibility, 70
constituency
   judgment of leadership, 111
   modeling behavior for, 58
   relating to, 68
   watchfulness of, 55
counterproductivity, 55
creating leaders, 1

decision-making, 6
decisiveness, 40–41
delegation, 90–92, 117
derailing, 56
developing, 82, 117–118, 124–125
   sticking points, 85
   tenets, 133–134
   uniqueness of power, 83
development
   and balance, 93–94
   of leaders, 2, 6
   leadership and personal, 1
development plan, 136–137
dimensions, 93–95
disposition, 3
doers, 3

effectiveness, of leaders, xii, 1, 8–9
empowerment, and delegation, 90
energy, 38
   focusing, 37
   generating, 32–33
   plugging leaks in, 44–45, 114
envisioning, 24–25, 27
equations, 7–8, 12
   Leadership Capacity, 112
"everything to everyone" trap, avoiding, 42–45
expectations, on leaders, 13–14
expenditures, replenishing, 48

failure, xiii
fall-back strategies, 64
fallibility, demonstrating, 75–76
5 Powers, 18

focus, 36, 114, 121–122
  through anticipation, 46–47
  definition of, 37
  and energy leaks, 44–45
  "nothing else matters," 40–41
  sticking points, 39
  tenets, 130–131
followers, 2

gardens, of China, 59–60
the glue
  acknowledging effort, 81
  anticipation, 47
  balanced development, 94
  best effort standard, 57
  communicating a vision, 29
  cultivating agility, 65
  definition of, 12
  delegation, 92
  envisioning, 27
  extracting takeaways, 87
  grow continually, 96
  inspiration, 31
  integrity, 63
  multidimensionality, 79
  narrowing focus, 41
  perspective building, 60
  plugging energy leaks, 45
  productive attitude, 55
  removing egotism, 76
  replenishment, 49
  resource leader, 43
  stepping out, 74
  thinking abundantly, 89
  urgency, 33
  values, 35
  visibility, 72
goals, defining
gray zones, 64, 115
G2. *See* the glue

heart, following, ix–x

inclusion, standardizing, 81
inspiration, and vision, 30–31
integrity
  operating with, 61–63
  reasons for lack of, 62–63
integrity breaches, 61–62
intoxication, with "position," xiii
introspection, and integrity, 63

Kyra, insight of, ix

leaders,
  as anticipators, 46–47
  and approach to life, 48
  common deficiencies, 67
  creation of, 1
  effectiveness of, xii, 1, 8–9
  example setting, 87
  expectations for, 13, 51
  fallibility of, 75–76
  pressures on, 8
  qualities of, xii, 54
  reasons for failure of, xiii
  responsibility to constituency, 30
  visibility of, 70–72
leadership
  and abuse of position, xiii
  challenges to, 119
  closing thoughts on, 120
  concerns about, 6
  and effort, 57
  and egotism, 75–76
  energy requirements, 37–38
  and gray zones, 64–65
  identifying, xii
  Kyra's insights on, ix
  lifelong nature of, 2

and management, 3
philosophical perspectives on, 1–3
poor, xiv
like a puzzle, xi
versus management, xiii, xiv
potential for, xi
success, sharing of, 80
Leadership Capacity (LC), 111–112
   definition, xvii
   scorecard, 135
leadership development, 52
   common beliefs about, 6–7
   equational relationships, 7–8
   life-balance approach to, 83
   and organizations, 9
Leadership Development Tool, 127–137
   instructions for, 128
leadership puzzle, xi
leaks, energy, 44–45
learning, and leadership, 86–87
L5 model, 18
life, holistic approach to, 48
life-balance approach, to leadership development, 83
limitations, appreciating, 42–43

macro vision, 23–24
management
   integrity levels of, 61–62
   and leadership, 3
   versus leadership, xiii, xiv
managing, 78
mentoring, 77, 78
micro vision, 24–25

negative comments, effects of, 62
"nothing else matters," 40–41

opportunity, creating, 15, 88–89
organizational crisis, equational relationships, 7–8
organizations
   and leadership development, 9
   necessary investments, 6
   reliance on leadership, 2–3

paradoxes, 8, 49
   of development, 83
perfection, fallacy of, 75–76
perserveration, avoiding, 40
personal development wheel, 95
perspective, and agility, 64
perspective building, 58, 115
philosophy, of leadership, 1–3
pie metaphor, 88–89
planning. *See* anticipation
power, abuse of, xiii
Powers
   attitude, 50–65
   developing, 82–96
   focus, 36–49
   main points. *See* sticking points
   relating, 66–81
   vision, 19–35
   see also individual Powers
pressures, on leaders, 8
psychological hardiness, 52
puzzle
   as leadership analogy, xi

questions
   on awareness, 15
   on best effort, 56
   on envisioning, 27
   about leadership, xii
   for scenarios, 98
   about vision, 32

relating, 66, 116–117, 123–124
  definition of, 67
  evaluation of, 68
  by stepping out, 73–74
  sticking points, 69
  tenets, 132–133
resource availability, 88–89
resource leader, 43
retreats, micro-level vision, 24
reverse-delegating, 91

scale, for Leadership Development Tool, 128
scarcity mentality, 89
scenarios
  aggressive leadership (Alex), 105–109
  heated exchange (Robert), 99–104
sideline leadership, 13
SMART, 94
stakeholders, and vision delivery, 28
stepping out, 73–74
sticking points, 113–118, 121–125
  attitude, 53
  definition, xvii
  developing, 85
  focus, 39
  relating, 69
  vision, 26
strategies, for delegation, 91–92
success
  and attitude, 52
  components of, xiv
  measuring, 111–112
  sharing, in, 80–81
sustainability issues, and leadership effectiveness, xii

takeaways, extracting, 87
tank-filling activities, 48–49
teams, and perspective, 59
teamwork, emphasizing, 80
time, as leadership requirement, 37
timing, 70

unprepared leader, xiv
urgency, and vision, 33

values, and vision, 34
vertical building, 80–81
visibility, 70–72, 116
vision, 19, 27, 113
  communicating, 28–29
  definition of, 20
  levels of, 20–21
  macro level, 23–24
  micro level, 24–25
  sticking points, 26, 121
  tenets, 130
  see also envisioning
vision ring, *22*

waiting (anecdote), 73–74
weakness, and relating, 67–68

978-0-595-39606-1
0-595-39606-2

Printed in the United States
76432LV00007B/223-231